3765302?

Terry N<

B GEORGE v±

George VI : the dutiful
king

D0948429

Bond Book ☑

This book is part of a special purchase plan
to upgrade the CALS collection. Funds for
the project were approved by Little Rock
voters on 7/14/15. Thanks, Little Rock!

Penguin Monarchs

THE HOUSE OF TUDOR

Henry VII	Sean Cunningham
Henry VIII	John Guy
Edward VI	Stephen Alford
Mary I	John Edwards
Elizabeth I	Helen Castor

THE HOUSE OF STUART

James I	Thomas Cogswell
Charles I	Mark Kishlansky
[Cromwell	David Horspool]
Charles II	Clare Jackson
James II	David Womersley
William III & Mary II	Jonathan Keates
Anne	Richard Hewlings

THE HOUSE OF HANOVER

George I	Tim Blanning
George II	Norman Davies
George III	Amanda Foreman
George IV	Stella Tillyard
William IV	Roger Knight
Victoria	Jane Ridley

THE HOUSES OF SAXE-COBURG & GOTHA AND WINDSOR

Edward VII	Richard Davenport-Hines
George V	David Cannadine
Edward VIII	Piers Brendon
George VI	Philip Ziegler
Elizabeth II	Douglas Hurd

PHILIP ZIEGLER

George VI
The Dutiful King

ALLEN LANE
an imprint of
PENGUIN BOOKS

ALLEN LANE

Published by the Penguin Group
Penguin Books Ltd, 80 Strand, London WC2R ORL, England
Penguin Group (USA) Inc., 375 Hudson Street, New York, New York 10014, USA
Penguin Group (Canada), 90 Eglinton Avenue East, Suite 700, Toronto, Ontario,
Canada M4P 2Y3 (a division of Pearson Penguin Canada Inc.)
Penguin Ireland, 25 St Stephen's Green, Dublin 2, Ireland (a division of Penguin Books Ltd)
Penguin Group (Australia), 707 Collins Street, Melbourne, Victoria 3008, Australia
(a division of Pearson Australia Group Pty Ltd)
Penguin Books India Pvt Ltd, 11 Community Centre, Panchsheel Park,
New Delhi – 110 017, India
Penguin Group (NZ), 67 Apollo Drive, Rosedale, Auckland 0632, New Zealand
(a division of Pearson New Zealand Ltd)
Penguin Books (South Africa) (Pty) Ltd, Block D, Rosebank Office Park,
181 Jan Smuts Avenue, Parktown North, Gauteng 2193, South Africa

Penguin Books Ltd, Registered Offices: 80 Strand, London WC2R ORL, England

www.penguin.com

First published 2014
001

Copyright © Philip Ziegler, 2014

The moral right of the author has been asserted

All rights reserved
Without limiting the rights under copyright
reserved above, no part of this publication may be
reproduced, stored in or introduced into a retrieval system,
or transmitted, in any form or by any means (electronic, mechanical,
photocopying, recording or otherwise) without the prior
written permission of both the copyright owner and
the above publisher of this book

Set in 9.5/13.5 pt Sabon LT Std
Typeset by Jouve (UK), Milton Keynes
Printed in Great Britain by Clays Ltd, St Ives plc

ISBN: 978-0-141-97737-9

www.greenpenguin.co.uk

MIX
Paper from
responsible sources
FSC® C018179
www.fsc.org

Penguin Books is committed to a sustainable
future for our business, our readers and our planet.
This book is made from Forest Stewardship
Council™ certified paper.

Contents

CENTRAL ARKANSAS LIBRARY SYSTEM
ADOLPHINE FLETCHER TERRY BRANCH
LITTLE ROCK, ARKANSAS

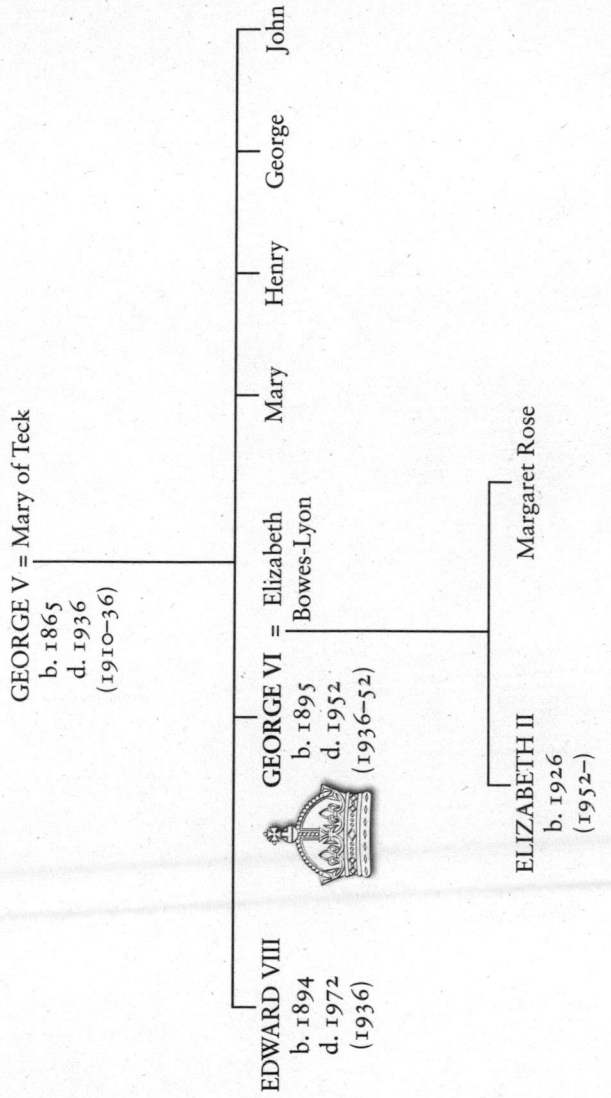

GEORGE V = Mary of Teck
b. 1865
d. 1936
(1910–36)

EDWARD VIII
b. 1894
d. 1972
(1936)

GEORGE VI = Elizabeth
b. 1895   Bowes-Lyon
d. 1952
(1936–52)

Mary   Henry   George   John

ELIZABETH II
b. 1926
(1952–)

Margaret Rose

George VI

I
Youth

If Ethelred was notoriously 'Unready' and Alfred 'Great', King George VI should bear the designation of 'George the Dutiful'. Throughout his life he dedicated himself to the pursuit of what he thought he ought to be doing rather than what he wanted to do. Inarticulate and loathing any sort of public appearance, he accepted that it was his destiny to figure regularly and conspicuously in the public eye, gritted his teeth, largely conquered his crippling stammer and got on with it. Deeply conservative with a small 'c' and, if he had been free to vote, with a capital 'C' as well, he realized that he must work with the Labour ministers of 1945 and win their trust and respect. Ferociously short-tempered, he learned not merely to suffer fools gladly but to remain calm in the face of what he sometimes felt was almost intolerable provocation. Home-loving and not deriving from travel the intellectual stimulus which some people find in it, he nevertheless resignedly undertook laborious journeys around the world in the service of his country. A passionate imperialist, he presided with only muted complaint over policies which he realized must lead to the disintegration of the British Empire. It was, in many ways, a ghastly life; yet at least he could tell himself that he had never failed to do his duty.

Like many of Britain's more estimable monarchs, he was not born to be king. He was a second son, doomed by his royal birth to occupy a prominent position yet spared the ultimate burden of the crown. And on 14 December 1895, when Prince Albert Ferdinand Arthur George was born at York Cottage, a house in the grounds of Sandringham in north Norfolk, that burden was indeed heavy. The powers of the monarchy had been dwindling for several hundred years but its influence was still formidable. Queen Victoria, the baby prince's great-grandmother, took it for granted that it was her right to be informed of any development of importance in her realm and was affronted if her opinion was ignored. She was grandmother to half the crowned heads of Europe and presided over the most extensive and richest empire that the world had ever seen. In the long years of seclusion that had followed the death of her beloved husband, Albert, the monarchy had to some extent lost favour with the people but now, in her extreme old age, the rare appearances of that tiny dumpy figure, swathed always in the blackest mourning, commanded extravagant respect and interest. That tired old cliché – 'a legend in her own time' – might have been coined for Queen Victoria.

To be the great-grandson of a living legend is a daunting proposition. Bertie, as he was generally called, had further problems. His grandfather, the Prince of Wales and future King Edward VII, was mildly alarming but on the whole benevolent. His father, then Duke of York and eventually King George V, was a more daunting figure: a martinet of limited intelligence and negligible imagination who had spent his most formative years in the Royal Navy and never shed the rigid mindset and conventional ideas that are traditionally associated with military service.

Bertie got off to a bad start when he was born on the day on which Prince Albert had died in 1861. His parents expected outraged protests from the queen and apologized nervously for their solecism: to their relief she took the matter calmly and even wrote in her diary that she felt it might be 'a blessing for the dear little boy and may be looked upon as a gift from God!' She thoroughly approved the proposal that the baby should be named Albert, consented to act as godmother and even gave him a bust of the Prince Consort as a christening present.

Bertie's mother had been born Princess Mary of Teck – a family grand enough by most standards but insignificant when compared to the British royal house. She was better educated than her husband and possessed what to most people seemed a dominant personality, but her father, the Duke of Teck, was not deemed to be of royal blood and she was acutely conscious of the fact that she was descended from a morganatic marriage. As a result, she viewed her husband's family connections with exaggerated deference. She had previously been engaged to the Duke of York's elder brother, Prince Eddy, an effete and debauched profligate who, luckily both for her and for his country, developed pneumonia and died in 1892. Princess Mary's hand in marriage and, as it fortunately turned out, her affections, were briskly transferred to the younger brother. The marriage was a complete success; the only pity was that her reverence for the British monarchy led to her rarely standing up to her husband and allowing him to set the tone in their relationship with their children.

The results were regrettable. The Duke of York was neither cruel nor unfeeling and while his children were infants he treated them with almost doting affection. As they grew up and began to show signs of independence, however, the martinet took over. As a midshipman he had been subjected to the strictest discipline, denied luxuries or even modest comforts, expected to conform in every way. He treated his children as midshipmen, both before they had attained that status and long after they had put it behind them. Fortunately for them he was able to devote relatively little time to their affairs; few children in upper-class families saw much of their parents, royal children saw less than most.

His wife dutifully followed his example. The Duchess of York in later life earned the reputation of being remote and somewhat chilly. Her elder son, as Duke of Windsor, did all he could to promote this view. 'I am afraid,' he wrote after she died in 1953, 'the fluids in her veins have always been as icy cold as they are now in death.'[1] But the letters he wrote to her when he was a young man tell a different story: he spoke of 'cosy and confidential talks ... It's so wonderful to feel that we can really talk things over, and vital and *intime* things.'[2] Her problem was not that she lacked feeling but that she was bad at showing it. Reticent by nature, her inhibitions were reinforced by her husband's conviction that displays of emotion should be reserved for the strictest privacy or, better still, eschewed altogether. Her relationship with her children tended to be formal: Bertie respected his mother, in a way loved her, but did not feel towards her the instinctive warmth that can be taken for granted in most such relationships.

*

He was, from the start, outshone by his elder brother. David was quicker, funnier, more attractive and very conscious of the fact that he was the senior. When, two years later, a daughter, Mary, was added to the family, Bertie receded still further into the background. He was not unhappy as a result but he signally failed to grow in confidence. Whether this lack of confidence caused him to stammer or his stammer fed his lack of confidence, it was at this stage in his life that he developed the crippling handicap that was to make much of his life so burdensome. It did not help that he was naturally left-handed yet, as was the custom of the time, was forced to write with his right hand. In speech, certain letters or syllables regularly defeated him: he could see them coming, desperately sought circumlocutions to avoid them, usually failed and became bogged down in interminable pauses as he tried vainly to bring out the offending word. For anyone it would have been a torment; for Bertie, knowing that he was bound to spend much of his life in the public eye, it was doubly horrible. His father made matters worse by treating the affliction as a weakness which could be overcome with a little determination. 'Get it out, boy!' he would bark angrily as the wretched child struggled to complete a sentence. When to this trouble were added knock knees, which were countered by forcing him to wear splints uncomfortable at best, painful at worst, and in either case degrading – the miracle is that Bertie grew up not a yammering imbecile but a determined, lively and on the whole well-balanced boy.

Most of his childhood was spent at York Cottage. Harold Nicolson uncharitably described it as a 'glum little villa'.[3]

A villa it was perhaps, but it is large enough today to provide spacious estate offices, storage rooms for the Sandringham shop and five decent-sized flats. It was cosy and unpretentious: qualities which suited the Duke of York. Nor, for Bertie, was it in the least 'glum': for him it was home – a concept which he found difficult to attach to the ever more palatial residences in which he was destined to spend his life.

At first he was in the charge of governesses; then, in 1902, the year after Queen Victoria died and his father became Prince of Wales, it was decided that it was time for him and his brother to put aside childish things. A tutor was imported to supervise the process: Henry Hansell, a schoolmaster by profession. Hansell was honourable, diligent and kindly but with only the most rudimentary sense of humour and almost entirely without imagination. He represented everything that was most philistine and blinkered about the English upper-middle classes. Prince Bertie would never have been an intellectual or an aesthete, but under different direction he might at least have been alive to a world not wholly circumscribed by games, shooting and the demands of daily life. Even in imparting the rudiments of an academic education, Hansell was deficient. Bertie was consistently bottom or very near the bottom in every examination that he had to take. He was far from being a fool – he possessed common sense and a fine ability to distinguish between the trivial and the important, the spurious and the authentic – but under Hansell's well-meaning guidance he grew bored and restless and learned to identify education with everything that was most tedious and stultifying. To be fair to Hansell, he realized his own limitations and went as far as he dared in urging that his charges should be sent to some elite preparatory school. The Prince of Wales would have none of it: he had enjoyed private tutors himself and look how well he had turned out! If Bertie was not profiting by the regime, then it must be because he was stupid or idle, perhaps both. Anyway, his future was marked out and left no place for irrelevancies like preparatory or public schools. He was to serve in the Royal Navy. In January 1909, a few weeks after his fourteenth birthday, Prince Bertie was enrolled as a cadet in the Royal Naval College of Osborne on the Isle of Wight.

For any child to leave home for the first time must be a daunting experience. For a fourteen-year-old who had met scarcely any boys of his own age to be thrust into a world inhabited almost exclusively by his contemporaries must have added a touch of agony to the experience. To be a grandson of the king put the cap on it. The instructions were that Prince Albert was to be treated exactly like any other cadet. In practice his fellow pupils viewed him as a freak. On the one hand they itched to put him in his place, to show him that, at Osborne, being royal counted for nothing. On the other, they were uneasily aware that the divinity that hedged a king reflected some glory too on the king's grandson and, more practically, that his acquaintanceship might prove very valuable in the future. His older brother, with his quick wits and easy charm, had survived the experience without too much stress; for Bertie, gauche, shy and stammering, his first months at Osborne must have been almost unbearable.

He bore them because he knew that he had to. It is

doubtful that he ever conceived the idea of giving up – if he had done so he would at once have dismissed it as being a dereliction of duty too outrageous even to contemplate. He weathered the storm because he was so obviously unassuming and anxious not to play the prince; because he was good at games, which won him the respect of his contemporaries; and because he was of a friendly nature and always ready to think the best of anyone. He was never going to excel, to head the list in any popularity poll or be voted 'cadet most likely to succeed', but he was accepted as a decent and straightforward boy whose curiosity value soon wore off and who was generally felt to have fitted in.

To be accepted by his contemporaries was one thing; to meet the demands of the college was another. The fruits of Hansell's disastrous schooling were now evident. Prince Albert could write clear and comprehensible English, he knew a smattering of history and enjoyed learning more about the doings of his ancestors, but when it came to the skills with which Osborne was particularly concerned – mathematics, science and the like – he was conspicuously incompetent. Again and again he came bottom or almost bottom of the class, his inadequacy on paper being compounded by his stammer, which left his masters thinking that he was not merely ill-informed but slow-witted as well. It was almost inconceivable that a prince of the blood royal, still less one who was so high in the line of succession, should be dismissed from Osborne. If he had been anyone else, however, it is at least possible that he would have been judged inadequate and sent packing. Probably in such an event he would have ended up in the Brigade of Guards, where intellectual ability was not deemed a high priority for would-be officers.

It was some way into his second year at Osborne that his grandfather, King Edward VII, died suddenly and unexpectedly. Prince Albert was with his elder brother in London at the time, staying at Marlborough House, and the first news he had of his grandfather's death came when he saw the Royal Standard over Buckingham Palace flying at half mast. He mentioned this to his father, who muttered, 'That's all wrong' and ordered that the Standard should be transferred to Marlborough House and flown 'close up'. Edward VII might be dead but George V was now on the throne – the king lived. Prince Albert had been fond of his grandfather but the relationship had never been close; he felt grief, certainly, but the transformation of his father into king was something far more immediate and awe-inspiring.

With the funeral of King Edward VII behind him, Cadet Prince Albert returned to Osborne to prepare for the exams that he would have to take before he moved to Dartmouth on the next stage of his naval career. For most cadets they were something of a formality, but as the testing time approached it became alarmingly evident that the prince was not going to do well and might fail altogether. Not merely did he know very little; under the pressure of examination he found it difficult to concentrate and to assemble what he *did* know on paper. The reports on his progress were 'not at all satisfactory', protested his dismayed father. 'You don't seem to take your work at all seriously, nor do you appear to be very keen about it. My dear boy, this will not do.'[4] He was currently ranked seventy-first out of seventy-one. He seems temporarily to have made matters better, but the improvement did not last. Sixty-eight boys passed into Dartmouth and of these Prince Albert was sixty-eighth. Whether, if he had been anyone else, only sixty-seven boys would have passed into Dartmouth will never be known; this anyway was the nadir of his academic life. He made a poor start at his new college but never sank quite to the bottom and did progressively better as his stay at the naval college wore on.

It is only fair to say that he had to grapple with distractions which would not have affected any other cadet. One such was his father's coronation. Prince Albert, in naval uniform, rode in a carriage with his elder brother. The pomp, the circumstance, the realization that this was not just an English, not just a British, but an imperial occasion, affecting vast territories all around the world, strongly appealed to the impressionable prince. Not many people, contemplating that phlegmatic exterior and the apparent lack of interest in what was going on around him, would have suspected that he was deeply moved by the occasion; yet as the crown was placed on his father's head he experienced a sensation of awed excitement which surprised him by its potency. The occasion, too, lent a new dimension to his feelings for his brother. He had always acknowledged David's superiority – in charm, in ability and by right of birth; now, as King George V was crowned, he accepted that his brother, in future Prince of Wales, was a man apart. They would continue to be close friends, they would communicate with total freedom, but nothing could alter the relationship between them: for Prince Albert, henceforward, his brother would enjoy a flavour of the divine.

After such solemnities, returning to the parish pump activities of the naval college must have seemed unexciting. Prince Albert, though, buckled down with commendable zeal to making up for lost time and ensuring that he left Dartmouth, not in glory certainly but also not in disgrace. His final ranking – sixty-first out of sixty-seven – was hardly impressive but was significantly better than anything he had achieved before. Though those around him were hardly aware of it, he had turned a corner. The next six months, in which he completed his term as a naval cadet, were among the most formative of his life. In the final training cruise aboard HMS *Cumberland* he for the first time put behind him the routine of lectures and classrooms that he had found so irksome. He was doing work he enjoyed and for which he was fully competent; both physically and spiritually he throve in this novel atmosphere. The trip, however, provided less welcome reminders that though he was, in theory, a cadet like any other, in practice he was also a son of the king. In the West Indies and still more in Canada he was not allowed to shelter in the anonymity of the cadets' mess room but was forced to accept the well-meant but unwanted attentions of the local dignitaries. His captain did his best to shelter him but could not succeed entirely without causing grave offence. Shy and reticent, the prince found the experience disagreeable, but, as he had done in the darkest days at Osborne, he accepted that there was no escape. He lacked, and was always to lack, his brother's social charms but he found that he could do well enough; his success fed his self-confidence and gave him a new maturity which was immediately apparent to his father when he got back to England. The king visited *Cumberland* at the end of the naval manoeuvres which followed the tour. To the officer responsible for overseeing Prince Albert's progress he said simply: 'Thank you. I am pleased with my boy.'

On 15 September 1913 Prince Albert was appointed midshipman. His training was at an end. He was now to embark on his career as a naval officer which, he assumed, would be at the centre of his future life.

2
Duke of York

Within a year of Prince Albert's appointment Britain was at
war with Germany. Over the next few years he would be
trying to kill a strikingly large number of his cousins, and
equally they would be trying to kill him. The reflection does
not seem seriously to have disturbed him: he had met quite
a lot of his German relatives but none was among his closer
friends, his command of the language was no more than
adequate, he had never been to Germany and felt no real
affinity with its culture. His feelings at the outbreak of war
seem to have been those of most young men at the time:
excitement, a measure of apprehension, an assumption that
it would all be over in a matter of months. Army officers
leaving for France took with them evening dress so that
they would have something suitable to wear when they got
to Berlin. As a midshipman aboard the battleship HMS
Collingwood Prince Albert could hardly have hoped to
share this experience, but the question that most preoccupied him was whether he would have a chance of seeing
action before the war came to a rapid end.

Even if the war lasted long enough, he had other obsta-
cles to overcome. While at Dartmouth he had been plagued
by a series of gastric complaints which had been at best

uncomfortable and debilitating, at worst crippling. He dismissed them as being no more than a temporary inconvenience and did his best to carry on as usual. Then, after only three weeks of war, he retreated to the sickbay with pains so violent that he could hardly breathe. Appendicitis was diagnosed and he was put ashore at Aberdeen to be operated on. All went smoothly and he hoped that he would quickly be back on normal duties, but it soon became obvious that his recovery was no more than partial and that it was by no means certain that he would ever be able to return to sea. At any time this would have been a blow to him; in wartime, when almost every young man of spirit longed to be actively engaged against the enemy, his fate seemed to him uniquely pitiable. 'I am longing and have been longing for centuries to get back to my ship,' he told his father's equerry, Bryan Godfrey-Faussett. As a consolation he was given a desk job in the Admiralty. This at least meant that he was allowed to wear uniform, but it did not appease his chagrin at being safely on land while his contemporaries on *Collingwood* were at sea with the prospect of engaging the enemy at any moment. Prince Albert was not outstandingly heroic – he felt the pangs of fear as acutely as any of his contemporaries – but his wish to be allowed to fight and if necessary die alongside his fellow midshipmen was unfeigned and passionately held.

He got his way. In February 1915 he was at sea again. It proved to be only a fleeting respite. For a few months, all went well; he thought his medical troubles were behind him, but the gastric problems returned, it was a return to hospital, in the view of the doctors he should never serve at sea again. The view was not one that he shared and his father sympathized with his feelings. In the end, a compromise was agreed – the prince would remain ashore, doing as much as he felt able to, but if the Fleet put to sea in circumstances which made a naval battle seem probable, or at least possible, then he would be allowed to rejoin *Collingwood*. To the Prince of Wales, fuming at GHQ while his friends and fellow officers were butchered on the Western Front, he seemed unfairly privileged. 'Oh God, it is unbearable to live this usual life of ease and comfort,' the prince protested, 'while you my dear old boy, and all naval and army officers, are toiling under unpleasant conditions, suffering hardships and running gt risks with your lives, for the defence and honour of England.'[1]

Prince Albert was less sure; he suspected that when the moment of truth arrived and *Collingwood* went into battle he would be betrayed and left behind. Perhaps, if his senior officers had known what was going to happen, they would indeed have contrived to keep him ashore. Fortunately for him, they did not. He was at sea at the end of May 1915 when the German fleet unexpectedly came out of port to confront the Royal Navy in the only serious naval battle of the war. Jutland was not a glorious victory – in terms of ships lost it could even be described as a defeat – but after it the Germans retreated to their base and never ventured out again. Prince Albert was not required to play a heroic or even active role. He was, indeed, little more than an observer. *Collingwood* emerged from the battle unscathed. She had been under fire, though; her guns had damaged a German battlecruiser; the prince could properly claim that he had taken part in a naval battle and had been in danger of his life. He felt particularly pleased that he had felt no fear himself: 'It was certainly a great experience to have been through,' he noted proudly in his diary.

His months of fretfulness on shore yielded at least one dividend in that, for the first time, he really got to know his father. By this time the relationship between the king and the Prince of Wales was frosty if not hostile. The prince found life at court insufferably starchy and boring and went there as little as possible. The king thought that his elder son was frivolous and potentially a libertine. Prince Albert's loyalties were divided. He admired his brother excessively and half agreed with him in his assessment of family life: Buckingham Palace, he wrote, was 'an awful prison . . . The parents have got funny ideas about us, thinking we are still boys at school.'[2] But he also revered the king and knew at heart that he was far closer to him than he was to his more volatile and self-indulgent brother. The king and Prince Albert shared an unwavering devotion to duty and a sense of the obligations they owed the nation. From time to time the prince might mildly deplore the existence of this burden but, unlike his older brother, he never seriously questioned the fact that he was destined to bear it throughout his life. 'You have always been so sensible and easy to work with,' the king told him, 'and you have always been ready to listen to any advice and to agree with my opinion . . . that I feel we have always got on very well together (very different to dear David).'[3] He *was* different to dear David and the differences were to become ever more apparent over the next decade.

*

His life was still blighted by recurrent bouts of gastric illness. Finally, at the end of 1917, the doctors decided to
adopt what to many had for years seemed the most obvious
course of action: to conduct a major operation. It worked:
there was always to be a slight question mark over his
health but for the next thirty years he was able to lead a full
and normal life. From the point of view of his career it was
just in time. Only a few weeks before the operation he had
transferred to the fledgling Royal Naval Air Service. It was
a bold decision, for it was only fourteen years since the
Wright brothers had made their epoch-making first flight
and set the science of aviation going. Flying, to most people,
still appeared a most hazardous means of progress; for a
member of the royal family to indulge in it was surprising,
if not unseemly. To the mild chagrin of his elder brother –
who considered that *he* was the adventurous member of the
family – Prince Albert learned how to fly and in due course
received his wings; from his point of view the only flaw
in this achievement was that he was forbidden to fly solo.
He never enjoyed flying – he found it both alarming and
uncomfortable – but he felt that it was something that he
ought to do and stuck at it until he achieved success.

By now the war was over. What should he do next? Left
to himself he would probably have stayed with the navy
and returned to sea, but he was not left to himself and never
would be. He must, his father declared, take on the duties
of a prince. 'My brother is so overwhelmed with work that
I am going to help him with it,' he told a naval friend. 'It is
really the best thing to do.'[4] Even the king admitted, however, that the pitifully inadequate education Prince Albert

had received, followed by a few years in the wartime navy, was not a satisfactory preparation for the sort of challenge he would henceforth be facing. The prince should spend a year at Cambridge, studying history and economics. Unfortunately, the king then took measures to ensure that this enlightened decision yielded the smallest possible results. Prince Albert would be accompanied by his younger brother, Henry, future Duke of Gloucester – thus ensuring that he would be constantly in the company of the only undergraduate in the University of Cambridge less interested than he in academic matters. Worse still, the two princes were to live not in college but in a private house a mile away: a provision that the king thought would give them greater freedom but, in fact, removed any possibility that they would make stimulating friends. So far Prince Albert had viewed life solely from the perspective of the palace or an officers' mess; his father's ill-judged decision meant that the chance to broaden those horizons had been lost.

Indeed, almost the only benefit that he gained from his time at Cambridge came from the companionship of Louis Greig. Greig was a Scottish doctor, some ten years older than the prince, whom he had first met at Osborne and who had remained close to him ever since and accompanied him to Cambridge as equerry. Greig was no more likely than the prince's few undergraduate acquaintances to open his mind to new and challenging ideas but he was a man of strong character, patient, honourable and resolute. He was genuinely fond of the man who was both his master and his charge but saw too the frailties that threatened to cripple the prince's development: the explosively bad temper which would suddenly overtake him and render him almost incapable of civil intercourse; his inability to accept defeat gracefully; his black depression in the face of minor set-backs. 'My principal contribution was to put steel into him,' Greig once observed.[5] The steel was there already, but it needed a firm yet friendly hand to polish it and to ensure that it showed always to best advantage.

The time had come for the prince to lend a hand in the work of monarchy. The gruesome fate of the Russian royal family had reminded everyone that the monarchical order was under extraordinary challenge. The republicans were vociferous; it was high time, H. G. Wells told readers of *The Times*, that the country rid itself of 'the ancient trappings of throne and sceptre'.[6] In Britain, at least, republicanism was more noisy than effective; what evidence there is suggests that only a very small proportion of Britons would have chosen to dispense with the monarchy. The king, however, took the threat most seriously and his disquiet infected the rest of the family. When the Habsburgs and the Hohenzollerns swiftly followed the Romanovs into oblivion, alarm grew close to panic. The Prince of Wales was despatched on a series of tours around the empire to improve his understanding of his future subjects and generally to boost the royal cause; Prince Albert was assigned to the home front.

The home front needed attention. Lloyd George's pledge to make Britain 'a land fit for heroes to live in' showed few signs of being fulfilled: working conditions in many of the factories were primitive, housing was overcrowded and insalubrious, hospitals and schools inadequate. Industrial relations became the prince's speciality and he proved to be both quick to learn and characteristically assiduous in his studies. He toured the country, endlessly enquiring and, by asking the right questions, provoking the right responses from the employers. 'Of all the many visitors we had here,' said one surprised factory manager after a royal inspection, 'I never met one who asked more sensible questions or showed greater understanding of our fundamental problems.'[7]

His interest was genuine; so also was his patently sincere belief that the gap between capital and labour, between employer and employed, was dangerously great and should as far as possible be reduced. He was no revolutionary. He believed that, in general, God had intended the rich man to be in his castle and the poor man at his gate. But that was no reason why the rich man should not treat the poor man with proper consideration and that there should not be regular intercourse between gate and castle. Particularly this was the case where the young were in consideration: Prince Albert believed that the young of all classes and income groups should be encouraged to mix together. Having reached this conclusion, he decided to do something about it. He conceived the idea of annual camps at which a hundred or so working-class boys would be invited to join the same number of public schoolboys at a site near the sea where they could swim, work, play games and, above all, get to know each other. He had to leave the organization and day-to-day running of the camps to others but he promoted the idea of them enthusiastically, raised money for them and paid them regular visits. If there is one image of the duke at this point which identifies him most clearly in the public mind it is the one which shows him in shorts and open-necked shirt sitting amid a crowd of boys, singing lustily and making the appropriate gestures that accompanied what became the signature tune of the camps, 'Under the Spreading Chestnut Tree'. It was home-spun stuff, far less sophisticated than anything the Prince of Wales would have considered undertaking, but it marked Prince Albert as the people's prince, decent, unpretentious, socially aware. It was a reputation which one day was to stand him in good stead.

On 3 June 1920 he was created Duke of York. 'I know that you have behaved very well in a difficult situation for a young man and that you have done what I asked you to do,' his father told him approvingly.[8] It became every day more apparent that, among the royal children, he was the one whom the king felt was closest to him and conformed most closely to his own image. It was an impression that was to be reinforced when, a few years later, the duke married a woman whom his father not merely felt was suitable but took enthusiastically to his heart.

It was probably the most important decision he made in his life, and certainly one of the most successful. Lady Elizabeth Bowes-Lyon (the hyphen came and went according to the whim of each member of the family) was the penultimate (and ninth) child of the Earl of Strathmore. The Strathmores were very grand. They had been living in their extravagantly be-turreted castle of Glamis since the fourteenth century and the 14th Earl, though he was far too good-mannered to say so, probably considered the Hanoverian immigrants

23

who inhabited Buckingham Palace to be nothing very special in the way of breeding. His daughter, Elizabeth, was intelligent, vivacious and exceptionally attractive. Like most upper-class girls of her generation her education had been erratic and individual: asked whether she could spell long words, she offered as examples of her knowledge 'capercaillie' and 'ptarmigan'.[9] Unlike most upper-class girls, however, she was encouraged to read and did so omnivorously; poetry, in particular, was important to her throughout her life.

She was just eighteen when the First World War ended and it was not until 1920 that the London season got under way again. Her impact was immediate and electric: she loved dancing and was exceptionally good at it; she relished company and enjoyed meeting new people; her radiant enthusiasm made her the sort of girl that everyone, however unsuited to the social scene, wanted to talk to and have as a friend. For the Duke of York she was the ideal companion; it did not take him long to conclude that she was also the girl he wanted to marry.

If he had been heir to the throne there might have been hesitation – for the future king to marry a commoner, however socially eligible, would have been an alarming precedent. For a second son, however, she was deemed entirely suitable. All the doubts were on her side. The duke proposed and was rejected; Lady Elizabeth saw too clearly the sacrifice of liberty she would have to make if she joined the royal family. In due course he tried again. 'You are one of my best and most faithful friends,' Lady Elizabeth assured him. 'I am too miserable about it.' Being a faithful friend was not at all what the duke had in mind. A less determined man might have abandoned the quest at this point but once again he demonstrated his resolve to achieve whatever he felt was right and proper. In the end he prevailed; Lady Elizabeth put aside her doubts and concluded that he was indeed the man with whom she wished to spend her life. They were married with much pomp in Westminster Abbey on 26 April 1923; everyone who was anyone was there, including fifty-two working-class boys, mainly from the East End, invited at the insistence of the duke.

After his death the Queen Mother, as she was from then onwards generally styled, used indignantly to protest whenever it was suggested that without her the duke would not have been able to carry out the duties imposed upon him. She was right in that, however painful he found it, the duke would have forced himself to carry on. But the cost to his health, both physical and mental, would have been enormous, he might have broken down under the strain – at the very least he would have done what he had to do with less ease and grace. She gave him confidence, she gave him strength; the supreme test was not to come for another thirteen years or so, but even in the period before his brother's abdication her role was of inestimable importance.

They began their married life at White Lodge, a substantial mansion in the heart of Richmond Park. In theory this offered the attraction of being secluded yet accessible to central London; in practice it was inconveniently far from those parts of the capital where most of their engagements took place and embarrassingly open to the scrutiny of friendly but importunate sightseers. The duke disliked it from the start, but it was four years before he managed to exchange it for a home in central London – 145 Piccadilly – where he was to remain until he came to the throne. It was from White Lodge that they set off on their first official tour overseas – to Belgrade for a royal christening and wedding – and it was still their base when, in 1927, they spent six months on a mammoth and gruelling tour of Australasia.

Excursions of this kind were doubly onerous for the duke because of the stammer, which still made public speaking an agonizing burden. It was never wholly cured: the author remembers, as a boy in the late 1930s, listening to the king on the radio painfully struggling to get out some difficult word, with the whole nation willing him to succeed. The handicap, and the gallantry with which he challenged it, in fact won him vast sympathy and admiration, but to him it spelled only humiliating failure. Painfully apparent though it still was, however, it was by then clearly far less crippling an affliction than it once had been. In 1926 the duke had put himself into the hands of Lionel Logue, a more or less self-taught Australian speech therapist who had set up shop in London. 'He entered my consulting room,' wrote Logue, 'a slim quiet man with tired eyes and all the outward symptoms of the man upon whom habitual speech defect had begun to set the sign. When he left at five o'clock, you could see that there was hope once more in his heart.'[10] There was no miraculous overnight cure, but Logue taught him how to control his breathing and convinced him that, if he worked at it, improvement was not only possible but inevitable.

*

The duke and his elder brother had grown further apart during the inter-war years; in so far as he mixed at all with members of his family, the Prince of Wales was more likely to choose his youngest surviving brother, George, who in 1934 became Duke of Kent. There was no quarrel between the brothers, merely recognition of the fact that their tastes had little in common, and that they viewed life, both public and private, from a very different point of view. The Prince of Wales found Bertie decidedly dull: worthy, no doubt, but not stimulating company. The gulf widened after the duke's marriage: the Duchess of York liked and, up to a point, enjoyed the company of her brother-in-law and shared her husband's admiration for him, but she knew that they and the duke were on different paths and had no doubt that theirs was the better one. They grew no closer when the Yorks produced a family: Princess Elizabeth in April 1926 followed by Margaret Rose in 1930. The popular press portrayed the Prince of Wales as a regular visitor at 145 Piccadilly, romping with his infant nieces in the nursery. 'Uncle David in our nursery!' exclaimed Princess Margaret many years later. 'I don't think he ever got there. Well, perhaps once he did.'[11]

From the point of view of the Duke of York the most worrying feature of his brother's life was his failure to marry and produce an heir. This was something that was going to affect his daughter far more than him. He and the Prince of Wales were of much the same age; the prince seemed the more healthy of the two – even if the elder brother remained a bachelor and died first there was no reason to believe that the younger would long survive him.

For Princess Elizabeth, however, the threat of many years on the throne was very real. To some, no doubt, that would have seemed not a threat but an inviting prospect. The Duke of York, however, believed that he himself would be inadequate for the role and that to expect his daughter to become queen would be to lay an intolerable burden on her shoulders.

The only satisfactory solution was for the Prince of Wales to find a suitable wife and thus secure the succession. But the chances of this happening seemed ever more remote. The duke had rather liked his brother's first serious mistress, Freda Dudley Ward, but quite apart from the fact that she had a husband living she was clearly out of the question as a future queen. Since then things had gone downhill. Thelma Furness, pretty, sprightly, frivolous and born a Vanderbilt, was even more impossible. Her friend and successor as *maîtresse en titre*, Wallis Simpson, presented what must surely be the pinnacle of horror, by having not only a husband living but a divorce in her past as well. She surely would not last but what, the Yorks must have asked themselves, would come next? Shades of the throne were beginning to close around the mercifully unaware princess.

3
Abdication

Even as late as the beginning of 1936, the Duke of York found it impossible to believe that, when it came to the point, his brother would not shed Wallis Simpson, or at least relegate her to a background role. Most of the British Establishment shared this illusion. It is held by some that several months before the Prince of Wales acceded to the throne Baldwin, the prime minister, Lang, the Archbishop of Canterbury, and other such dignitaries had decided that he had no long-term future as monarch and must be manoeuvred into retirement. This is patently not the case. Baldwin, in particular, had formed a favourable impression of the prince when they had travelled together in Canada and elsewhere. Until long after such hopes had ceased to be realistic he continued to believe that the prince would finally be induced to put his country before his love. Like the Duke of York, he could not encompass the idea that anyone in their proper mind would set aside the glories and responsibilities of the throne to indulge a private passion. The Prince of Wales, of course, was *not* in his proper mind: he was blindly, besottedly in love in a way beyond the comprehension of his more temperate brother.

The trouble was that the Prince of Wales believed that he

had the right to a private life and that what he did with it was his own affair. His brother, more realistically, knew that the monarch could have no private life, or at least none outside the intimate domesticity of his family. He viewed his brother's activities with disapproval and dismay. He did not refuse to meet the prince's mistress but he made a point of trying to avoid events when they might be together. On one occasion at least the Yorks were dining at the Dorchester when the Prince of Wales and Wallis arrived with another party. Unobtrusively, the Yorks left within a quarter of an hour.[1] From time to time they visited the prince in his hideaway of Fort Belvedere, but such occasions became increasingly rare and discreet enquiries would be made before they set out to establish whether Mrs Simpson would be present.

What was already a considerable embarrassment became calamitous when King George V died at Sandringham on 20 January 1936. His end was sudden. Some believe that the Prince of Wales was taken by surprise and that, if his father had survived for another year or two, he would have found a way of extracting himself from the line of succession and leaving the throne to the Duke of York. It is possible that he played with the idea but it seems unlikely that it went far beyond that; in any case it was too late – like it or not, he was now King Edward VIII.

Even without the unsettling presence of Mrs Simpson in the background there would have been squalls ahead. One of his admirers told him that he was 'the most modernistic man in Europe'. He took it as a compliment. His brother would have been dismayed if a similar charge had been levelled against him. The new king's nature was iconoclastic, he relished change for its own sake. The Duke of York viewed change with suspicion and a measure of distaste. In each individual case he would need convincing that it was really necessary and that the discarding of old practices and traditions would not create more problems than it solved. He did not openly criticize any of the new king's vigorous, if somewhat desultory, efforts to reform the running of the court – in his eyes that would have been disloyal – but his brother can have been in little doubt that the Duke of York was out of sympathy with the pattern of the new reign.

This was one of the reasons why he found himself increasingly distanced from the day-to-day running of the monarchy. He was not being kept in the dark about the affairs of government. On the contrary, he was shown most of the important official papers and was briefed regularly on affairs of state. Some even suspect that the king made a point of ensuring that his brother knew what was going on so as to prepare a way for his own eventual retreat. But the king himself rarely spoke to his brother about matters of moment; indeed, he rarely spoke to him at all. Apart from anything else, the king was almost entirely preoccupied by his own problems. He knew that any protracted conversation with the Duke of York was certain to turn to his relationship with Mrs Simpson, and he had no wish to see his family involved in such an issue. If he had to discuss the matter with anyone it would be with the prime minister; his mother and his brothers were left to fret in isolation.

Almost the only field in which the king did ask his brother to play an active role was in the reorganization of

Sandringham. It was inevitable that a large house, lavishly maintained, with an estate primarily important for its shooting, would cost a lot to run, but under George V the expenses had become exorbitant. The new king threatened to sell it – to the dismay of his brother, some of whose happiest times had been spent there. He then entrusted the Duke of York with the job of making it run more economically. The duke disliked the task but at least preferred it to the alternative of seeing Sandringham lost for ever. He set to work conscientiously and produced a long list of potential reforms, most of which were implemented when he himself became king. He was offered no similar opportunity at Balmoral, where Edward VIII unleashed a fusillade of ferocious economies, many of them at the expense of veteran servants of the estate. 'David only told me what he had done after it was over, which I must say made me rather sad,' the duke wrote wistfully to his mother.[2] He was to be sadder still before many months had passed.

Ironically, in view of what was to happen, one activity in which the king was anxious to involve his brother was planning for the coronation, which was to take place in 1937. The king was bored by ceremonies, particularly religious ones, and he disliked Cosmo Lang, the Archbishop of Canterbury, who would inevitably play a large part in the celebrations. It was not surprising that, after one token appearance at the Coronation Commission, he should have appointed his brother as chairman and washed his hands of the whole affair. In fact, most of the work was done by another body, the Coronation Joint Committee, which was run by the Duke of Norfolk; so though the Duke of York was more heavily involved than the king, it did not prove to be a particularly time-consuming exercise.

As 1936 wore on it became ever more evident that in the king's mind nothing was more important than his relationship with Mrs Simpson. The Yorks continued to stand aloof. When the king hired a yacht, the *Nahlin*, and cavorted for several weeks around the eastern Mediterranean, it was very evident that Mrs Simpson was a member of the party, equally noticeable that the Yorks were not. Nor did they make more than a token appearance at Balmoral. 'It is very sad,' the duchess told Queen Mary, 'and I feel this whole difficulty is a certain person. I do not feel that I can make advances to her and ask her to our house, as I imagine would be liked.'[3] Up till this time the king's affair with Mrs Simpson had been conducted more or less decorously and out of the public eye; but more and more he was thrusting it forward, as if he knew that the crisis must come sooner or later and for him sooner would be better. In September 1936 he was due to open a new hospital in Aberdeen. He cried off at the last minute on the plea of pressure of work and appointed his brother to act in his stead; then drove himself to Aberdeen to meet Mrs Simpson off the train.

After their Scottish season the Yorks returned to London to receive the dread news that Mrs Simpson's divorce would be heard at the end of October and that it would be unopposed. Until then the duke had clung to the belief that his brother would somehow pull back at the last minute, that the ultimate calamity would be averted. Now for the first time he accepted that marriage with Mrs Simpson was highly likely, if not yet quite inevitable; and that, if it took place, it would almost certainly involve the king's renunciation of the throne. Desperately he sought an opportunity to talk to his brother; surely it would still be possible to convince him of the error of his ways? 'He is very difficult to see,' he told Queen Mary sadly, 'and when one does he wants to talk about other matters.'[4] He set his thoughts out on paper: if the king took the trouble to read the letter he certainly paid no attention to it. When the Duchess of York joined in she gained no more success. 'Please be kind to Bertie when you see him,' she pleaded, 'because he loves you and minds terribly all that happens to you ... We want you to be happy, more than anything else, but it's awfully difficult for Bertie to say what he thinks, you know how shy he is – so do help him.'[5] Probably she expected no reply; certainly she got none.

It seems that even a week or two before the abdication the king was vacillating: not about whether he should marry Mrs Simpson – that was taken for granted – but whether he should brazen it out and maintain that he could both marry Mrs Simpson and retain the throne. At one point he actually insisted that, in such a case, Wallis Simpson should be queen, but in practice he seems to have envisaged the possibility of a morganatic marriage by which Wallis would become his wife but not his royal consort. He had powerful friends who urged such a course, Winston Churchill prominent among them. If the Duke of York had been personally responsible for deciding the government's position on such an issue, he would have been dreadfully perplexed. He was greatly concerned about his brother's happiness; he believed that Edward VIII, once he was free to concentrate on the task, would make an excellent monarch; he dreaded the thought of taking on a role for which he felt himself inadequate; and yet every sense he had of what was proper told him that the king would so degrade himself by marrying a twice-divorced American that he could not remain on the throne. Fortunately for him, he was hardly at all involved in the affair. Either through tact or because he was not particularly interested in the duke's view, Baldwin left him on the sidelines. It was the king himself who broke it to his brother that the die was cast: 'It looks to me now, the way things are shaping up, that I shall probably have to go.' The duke, according to his brother, was aghast. 'Oh,' he expostulated, 'that's a dreadful thing to hear. None of us wants that, I least of all.'[6]

On 8 December 1936 the Duke of York dined at Royal Lodge with the king and the prime minister. The king was in sparkling form, according to his admiring brother, telling Baldwin things about the conditions in the mining areas of south Wales of which the prime minister was unaware. 'And this is the man we are going to lose,' the duke murmured in awe to Walter Monckton, Edward VIII's most trusted adviser. He made one last futile effort to persuade the king to change his mind, then returned to London to break the news to his mother. 'When I told her what had happened,' he wrote, 'I broke down and sobbed like a child.'[7] But by now he had accepted the inevitable and resolved that he must go through with it. 'If the worst happens and I have to take over,' he had written a few days before, '. . . I will do my best to clear up the inevitable mess, if the whole fabric does not crumble under the shock and strain of it.'[8]

He believed that the whole fabric was indeed likely to crumble. He exaggerated the popularity of the king, exaggerated his doubts about his own inadequacy, underestimated the stability of the monarchy as an institution. He listened to his brother's farewell broadcast to the nation on 11 December, was profoundly moved by it, and felt that it was likely to provoke a wave of sympathy which would make his task impossible. The king's farewell was indeed poignant and touched many hearts, but the account of it which, in its chilling way, rings most true is that of the Conservative MP and socialite Chips Channon. Channon was dining with the Stanleys that evening and the party gathered around the radio to hear the words of the man who, a few hours before, had signed the Instrument of Abdication. 'It was a manly, sincere farewell,' wrote Channon. 'There was a stillness in the Stanleys' room. I wept, and I murmured a prayer for he who had once been King Edward VIII. Then we played bridge.'[9] For Britain too there was time for a tear and then it was back to the bridge table. The people accepted what had happened, deplored it, lamented briefly and then put the matter behind them and got on with life.

Part of that life was the new king, George VI. He found it hard to believe that he could carry it off. To his cousin, Louis Mountbatten, he poured out his doubts: he was unprepared for the job, he said, he had scarcely ever seen a state paper, his brother had had more than forty years to prepare for the role, he had no experience except that of a naval officer. Mountbatten was more than happy to offer consolation. By a curious coincidence, he said, the future King George V had called on Mountbatten's father when *his* elder brother, the Duke of Clarence, Prince Eddy, had died in 1892 and he had found himself abruptly transformed into the heir to the throne. Exactly like the new King George VI he had protested that he was unprepared for the role; all he knew in life was how to be a naval officer. 'George, you're wrong,' Mountbatten's father had replied. 'There is no more fitting preparation for a King than to have been trained in the Royal Navy.'[10] Whether or not George VI was wholly convinced by this reasoning, he seems to have found it comforting. History was to prove it true.

4
Becoming the King

It is undeniable that the abdication and the events leading up to it did less damage to the institution of monarchy than the new king feared would be the case, but harm was still done. The British people as a whole may have put the crisis behind them with striking speed, but there was an element among the politically conscious which was more concerned. It was estimated – by a staunch Conservative – that if a vote had been taken in the House of Commons at the end of 1936 at least a hundred members would have supported the establishment of a republic. One of these announced triumphantly: 'Since 1914 there has been a continual building up [of support] around the throne, but what has happened recently has done more for republicanism than fifty years of propaganda could do.'[1] When the new king asked his brother whether he imagined that it was a pleasure to take on a rocking throne and try to make it steady again he may somewhat have exaggerated the scale of the challenge, but nevertheless the challenge was real and urgent.

Where George VI did err was in underestimating his own capacity to deal with it. He had for so long been accustomed to esteem his elder brother as a miracle of charm and intelligence that he found it hard to believe he could successfully take his place. He rightly felt that he understood little of the mechanics of public life, knew few of the leading politicians personally and was singularly short of experience in foreign affairs; he also underestimated the extent to which common sense and a readiness to listen to the right advice could compensate for these deficiencies. In fact one of his problems was that, at the time of his accession, the right advice was hard to come by. He had inherited Alexander Hardinge as his private secretary and respected what he knew of him, but Hardinge had been overwhelmed by the pressures of the abdication and had retired hurt for a few months' travel in India. Alan – 'Tommy' – Lascelles was in time to become an indispensable member of the royal entourage, but at the beginning of 1937 he was still inexperienced and virtually unknown to his new employer. George VI was left with Clive Wigram as his counsellor and confidant. Wigram was no fool but he was of a different generation to the king and their temperaments were not easily compatible. To a striking extent the king was on his own, or would have been so if it had not been for the constant presence and support of the queen. She was no more versed than he was in public affairs but she had common sense, quick wits and a priceless ability to see things in proportion. Left to himself the king would have been prey to constant anxiety and indecision; with her by his side he knew his mind and expressed it with clarity and determination.

His first objective had clearly to be the re-establishment of the monarchy as the paradigm of all that was respectable and dignified in British life. Under Edward VIII the Palace had taken on a more raffish tinge – something alien both to the British people and to the disposition of the new king. George VI therefore needed to emphasize how different he was to his brother. Yet at the same time he knew that, though his people might dislike the idea of a court characterized by jazz, cocktails and Mrs Simpson, most of them knew little of the last king's train of life, did not really understand why he had gone and still felt considerable affection for him. If Edward VIII had not decided to go gracefully but instead had encouraged the establishment of a King's Party and had fought to retain both Mrs Simpson and the throne, he would not have prevailed, but he would have made things far more difficult for his brother. The thought that a considerable number of his subjects felt that his elder brother should still be on the throne did not make George VI any more confident as he addressed the problems ahead of him.

His trump card was his family. 'I know the people of this country,' said the former engine cleaner and now Labour MP J. H. Thomas. 'I *know* them. They 'ate 'aving no family life at Court.'[2] By the time of George's accession Princess Elizabeth was ten and her sister Margaret Rose six. They were attractive and photogenic children and pictures of the family, usually accompanied by a few dogs and the occasional pony, were standard fodder for the newspapers and magazines of the time. To suggest that the king consciously exploited his family so as to improve the image of the monarchy in the minds of the public would be to suggest mental processes totally alien to his character. He did not think in terms of publicity and images; if anyone had suggested that he should be preoccupied by such issues he would have been bemused and outraged. But he loved his own family in particular and believed that, in general, the united family must be at the heart of any stable society. He saw it as his duty to propagate that belief whenever he had an opportunity, and if exhibiting his own compact and contented unit to his people helped in that crusade, then he would not allow his own instinctive preference for privacy to weaken the effect.

One of the trickiest and in some ways most painful problems in the early years of George VI's reign – indeed, to some extent throughout his reign – was his relationship with his elder brother. The question was posed even before the new reign had properly begun. How, asked Sir John Reith, Director General of the BBC, should he introduce the former King Edward VIII before he made his farewell address to the people? Reith suggested 'Mr Edward Windsor'. With the common sense which marked his reign, George VI dismissed this idea as absurd. As the son of a duke his brother would anyway be Lord Edward Windsor. In that case he would, in theory, be able to stand for the House of Commons. If he were given an ordinary peerage he could sit in the House of Lords. Was this really what was wanted? Obviously he must become a royal duke; so Duke of Windsor he became.

But this was just the start of it. It was taken for granted by everyone who thought about the matter that the Duke of Windsor would leave the country for a while, and he did so with professions of goodwill on all sides. Things quickly turned sour. It became embarrassingly obvious that the duke had lied about the state of his finances, professing that he was far poorer than in fact he was and thus extracting a more generous allowance from his brother. The discovery never led to an open breach but it meant that George VI was far less sympathetic than he would otherwise have been when the expectations of the ex-king clashed with the facts of life in London. One of the first and most painful of these conflicts arose over the form of address for the former Mrs Simpson. The Duke of Windsor as a royal duke was automatically styled His Royal Highness. When Mrs Simpson married him – as she did in June 1937 – most people assumed that she would then too become HRH. She had her doubts, fearing the hostility of Queen Mary: 'York, guided by her, would not grant me the extra chic of creating me HRH.'[3] Her use of the word 'chic' in this context demonstrates vividly the gulf between her and her brother-in-law. It was a word of which George VI would hardly have been aware, still less have used about a matter which seemed to him of such moment. As it turned out, her doubts were justified – she never was formally granted the right to style herself HRH. Still worse, no member of the royal family attended their wedding; even Mountbatten, who at one point had volunteered himself as best man, found it inexpedient to make the journey.

The greatest bitterness, however, was generated by the duke's wish to return to Britain. He did not plan to have a permanent home there – at any rate not for several years; but he took it for granted that he would be free to visit this country, stay with friends and be received at court. The king saw things very differently. He believed that his brother's presence in Britain would automatically make him a focal point for a rival monarchy: 'You see, you can't have two Kings,' Queen Elizabeth, the Queen Mother, explained many years later.[4] This belief that the ex-king retained potent attractions for a substantial part of the British people was exaggerated from the start and became increasingly illusory as time wore on. It continued to haunt the king, however, long after it had become clear to everybody else that the new inhabitants of Buckingham Palace were firmly established on the throne.

An additional grievance of the Duke of Windsor was that, though the duke himself was told he would be welcome at the coronation, it was made clear that his wife would not be invited. Preparations for the coronation were already well advanced by the time of the abdication and it was decided that it would be better to stick to the agreed date – 12 May 1937 – rather than start the process all over again. Coronations were no more to George VI's taste than they had been to his elder brother's – processions and fancy dress, he accepted, were a necessary part of public life but should be kept to a minimum. The significance of the rite, however, he took with extreme seriousness: publicly to dedicate himself to the service of the nation was a sacred duty which he would perform with dignity and a certain reverence. His Christian faith was strong, if inarticulate: at the heart of the pomp and circumstance of the coronation was a simple religious ceremony; let those responsible dress up the rest of the affair with gorgeous pageantry, it was that intimate moment at which the Archbishop of Canterbury placed the crown on his head that to the king symbolized all that really mattered about the day's activities. It was a moment which he wished to share with his people; against the instincts of his more cautious advisers he insisted that the service should be broadcast and filmed for later exhibition. Left to himself he might even have allowed television cameras into the abbey, but the medium was very much in its fledgling days and he was persuaded without too much difficulty that this would be a step too far. All passed off well; one of the few setbacks occurred when one of the bishops trod on the king's robe, bringing him to an abrupt halt as he left the Coronation Chair. 'I had to tell him to get off it pretty sharply,' the king recalled in his account of the ceremony, a lively narrative which showed that, though he took the affair with proper seriousness, he was not beyond detecting the ridiculous in even the most solemn undertaking.[5]

If the king had had his way, the glories of the coronation would have been followed by the still more refulgent splendours of an Indian durbar. A visit to India had tentatively been planned for the winter of 1937–8 and George VI's imagination had been captured by the thought of being crowned king-emperor in this, the grandest and most populous of his territories. The viceroy, Lord Zetland, had at first strongly favoured the expedition, but as it seemed more and more likely that the Congress Party would take the opportunity of a royal visit to foment protest against British rule, he changed his mind and pressed for indefinite postponement. Ministers were disconcerted when the king took exception to the new advice. He *wanted* to go, he considered that the cancellation of the visit would be a sign of weakness on the part of the imperial power, he did not believe that there would be any serious disturbances in India or that his life would be in danger. He could not ignore the advice of his ministers but he made it clear that he thought them over-cautious and pusillanimous and that he was not disposed to accede automatically to advice that he thought ill-judged or that was contrary to his wishes.

It was one of the first indications that ministers had been given that the king had a mind of his own and was prepared to voice it emphatically. He was well aware of the constitutional limits to his role and would never strive to exceed them; equally, he knew his rights and would fight tenaciously to retain them. Ministers had grown unused to this. Edward VIII had been so preoccupied with his personal problems that he had taken little interest in the activities of his government: he had made fitful incursions – usually injudicious – into the world of foreign policy but had made no serious efforts to acquaint himself with, still less influence, the day-to-day activities of his ministers. Now they were confronted by a king who read his papers, formed opinions about them and did not hesitate to express those opinions forcibly. It was clearly a change for the better, but there were times when ministers hankered after the casual insouciance of the previous regime.

George VI was in temperament closer to his father. He was prudent yet determined, forming his own conclusions and, once having done so, slow to change them. He shared his father's obsession with detail, particularly when it came to points of dress: even the most distinguished officers of his court were likely to find themselves sharply rebuked if some medal ribbon was in the wrong place or a sartorial blunder had been committed. At a gillies' ball at Balmoral he sent for the pipe major and rebuked him for allowing one of the pipers to wear a kilt with the pleats pressed the wrong way. 'I noticed it as soon as I came into the ball-room,' said the king. But he was in general far more reticent than his father; he was more likely to listen to others than to air his own opinions. Conversation with him was never easy, partly because he had little use or aptitude for small talk, partly because he passed from topic to topic with disconcerting speed. Superficially he would seem – indeed was – unassuming but, again like his father, he never for a moment forgot that he was on the throne. Dignity, decorum, reliability were back; innovation and casual informality eschewed. 'Thus the Court, thank God, will revert to the old, well-tried ways,' wrote Canon Don, the archbishop's chaplain.[6] His relief would have been shared by almost any-one whose role it was to serve the monarchy.

George VI's first prime minister was Stanley Baldwin. Bald-win had played a large part in stage-managing the abdication. Some of his colleagues had doubts about the capacity of the Duke of York to replace his brother; Baldwin felt more sanguine, George would be just like his father, he told a colleague – than which he could hardly conceive higher praise. The two men were wholly compatible and if Baldwin had been five or ten years younger they would have formed a most harmonious partnership. As it was, however, he was resolved to retire as soon as the coronation was over. 'I would like you to know with what real sadness I accepted your resignation,' the king wrote to him; the words might have been written by any monarch to any prime minister, but there was real feeling behind them.

In his place came Neville Chamberlain, in some ways chipped off the same old block as his predecessor yet in character colder, less tolerant, more decisive. The king esteemed him from the start but did not at first feel the affection that had existed between himself and Baldwin. It was foreign affairs that convinced him that Chamberlain was not merely competent and safe but a heroic figure to be backed to the hilt. As Hitler's Germany became ever more belligerent and outrageous in its demands on its neighbours, those who influenced the making of policy in Great Britain fell ever more sharply into two camps: those who felt that Hitler should be confronted and checked, even at the risk of war, and those who believed that everything possible should be done to appease the dictator and persuade him to moderate his demands. No one who remembered the horrors of the First World War could be blamed for feeling that almost anything would be better than a return to arms. History today judges the appeasers to have been wrong. An opportunity, it is believed, was lost to stop Hitler before he was fully ready to go to war. At the time things seemed less clear: to many Churchill seemed an irresponsible warmonger and Chamberlain the voice of humanity and common sense. To support appeasement now seems to have been misguided, but those who did so then should not be condemned for cowardice or credulity; not many of us today can say with total confidence that we would have resisted its dulcet blandishments.

George VI was a convinced appeaser. He offered to intervene himself with a personal appeal to Hitler. When in September 1938 it seemed that the Germans were on the point of invading Czechoslovakia, he rejoiced when his prime minister flew to Germany to visit Hitler at Berchtesgaden and try to persuade him to hold his hand. When Chamberlain returned in triumph, flourishing his 'scrap of paper' and claiming that he had secured 'peace with honour ... peace in our time', the king was the first to praise him. Some thought that he went too far. If he had not been strongly discouraged by his advisers he would have gone to the airport to welcome Chamberlain home; as it was, he invited the prime minister to the Palace and appeared with him on the balcony. If a referendum had been held that night the vast majority of his subjects would probably have endorsed his conduct; within only a few months things looked very different.

However anxious the king might have been that war should be averted, he undertook two state visits in these years which directly contributed to the solidarity of what would one day be the alliance against Germany. The first, in July 1938, was to France. It seemed at one moment as if he might have to make the journey without the queen. Lady Strathmore died only a few days before the visit was due to start. Some frenzied pother followed; the queen, who was particularly close to her mother, must have been tempted to let her husband go to Paris alone but she knew how much he counted on her support. In the end the visit was postponed by some three weeks. It was fortunate for Anglo-French relations that this was done: the king alone would certainly have been well received but it was the queen who was the star of the show. Her beauty and her spontaneous charm made a startling impact on the notoriously unsusceptible Parisian crowd. The king had been well briefed as to what he should say. In all his public statements, he took pains to stress his hope that the international problems of the day would be solved by negotiation and goodwill. Many of the French who heard him may have considered that such hopes were slight; few if any can have foreseen that within two years victorious German troops would be marching along the Champs-Elysées.

The visit was complicated by the fact that the Duke of Windsor was now living in Paris and made it clear that he would take it much amiss if his brother did not call on him and include him in some at least of the official junketing. George VI, however, had been fed with a catalogue of offensive comments which the Duke and Duchess of Windsor were said to have made about the royal visitors. He was not disposed to reciprocate generously. 'State visit a most unsuitable moment for meeting,' he minuted. '. . . Official invitation would help their position in both countries . . . Their behaviour has not been polite to us.'[7] It is a sad comment on the relationship between the two brothers, who had once been so close, that the belief that an official invitation would help the Windsors' position in Parisian society was seen as a reason for not issuing one.

By the time that the king embarked on the second of his major trips abroad, to North America in May 1939, little hope was left that war might finally be averted. It did not seem possible that the United States could be induced to join a coalition against Germany, but it was essential that it should at least be well disposed towards the Anglo-French alliance and be ready to give it preferential treatment when it came to economic support and the supply of arms. The royal visit therefore formed part of a campaign to influence the hearts and minds of the American people. The operation had to be conducted with great delicacy. The American tour was presented as – indeed, was originally conceived as – an appendage to a royal visit to Canada. To avoid any accusation that the king was seeking to make political points he was accompanied, not by the British foreign secretary but by the Canadian prime minister. The visit was low-key, informal and yet designed to secure as much publicity as possible. It was largely due to the dexterity, as well as the obvious enthusiasm and goodwill, of the king and queen that the aims of the mission were accomplished.

The tour got off to an inauspicious start when the king's ship, *The Empress of Australia*, lost more than three days because of the inordinate number of icebergs along the route. The captain, the queen told Queen Mary, was driven almost demented by helpful passengers pointing out that his ship was close to the spot where, at much the same time of year, the *Titanic* had met its end. No such disaster occurred on this occasion and the visit to Canada was triumphantly successful. 'I realise now more than ever,' wrote the Governor General, Lord Tweedsmuir – more widely known as the novelist John Buchan – 'what a wonderful mixture [the king] is of shrewdness, kindliness and humour. As for the queen, she has a perfect genius for the right kind of publicity.'[8] That is the sort of thing governor generals are supposed to say, but there is enough evidence from other sources to suggest that Tweedsmuir's flattering words were fully justified.

The American public was a harder nut to crack. A large part of the population was both anti-imperialist and opposed to anything that they felt might embroil them in a European war. There was no overnight conversion as a result of the royal visit but in Washington they were greeted by enormous crowds, who may have come out of curiosity but, according even to the more anti-British elements of the American press, formed a most favourable impression of their visitors. What mattered more was the bond that was forged between the king and queen and President Franklin Roosevelt. They stayed with Roosevelt at Hyde Park, the president's family home on the Hudson River. The two men spoke long and seriously and George VI's record of their conversation reveals how frank the president was about the United States' attitude towards the forthcoming war and his hopes of influencing it in favour of the Allies. Indeed, he promised more than he was able to fulfil, for he told the king that, if the Germans were to bomb London, America would enter the war. A firm if unlikely friendship was established between the two men. For the five and a half years between September 1939 and his death in April 1945, Roosevelt, from the point of view of the future of Britain, was the most important man in the world. The fact that the king was able to write to him informally, reflecting the views of his government but in personal terms and free of the trammels of official communications, must, at the very least, have been a useful extra weapon in Britain's diplomatic armoury.

So it was back to Britain at the end of June, with Germany growing ever more belligerent and the inevitability of war becoming more obvious by the moment. George VI was one of the last people to abandon hope that Hitler might experience a last-minute change of heart. He offered, once more, to make a personal appeal; this time through his cousin, Prince Philip of Hesse. Chamberlain turned down the idea; he was probably right to do so, it would have achieved nothing and might merely have fortified Hitler in his belief that, when it came to the point, Britain and France would baulk at going to war.

That point came on 3 September 1939 when Germany invaded Poland. As his father had been a quarter of a century before, George VI found himself monarch of a country which was at war.

5
The King at War

What was a king supposed to do in wartime in the twentieth century? Clearly George VI was not going to lead his
troops into battle, nor was there really any role for him to
play in the direction of the war. Neville Chamberlain dutifully kept up the tradition of the weekly audience, but that
was the limit, and there were not many other links between
No. 10 and the Palace. Even in peacetime Chamberlain had
been apt to make decisions and take important actions
without reference to the king, sometimes leaving him to
find out what had happened through the press or wireless;
the extra demands on his time caused by the war meant
that the king was even more on the sidelines. Through other
sources, notably his private secretaries – Hardinge till July
1943 and after that Tommy Lascelles – the king was, however, exceptionally well informed. Scarcely anyone knew as
much as he did about the perils which his country was
facing and the inadequacy of its means of defending itself.
He was one of the handful of people who knew about Ultra,
the cracking of the German ciphers through a covert operation based at Bletchley Park – a secret so closely guarded
that it was nearly thirty years after the war was over before
any official admission was made of what had been achieved.

He read the Ultra transcripts, was sent the Cabinet minutes and a mountain of other secret and top-secret material, met and talked freely with many of those most responsible for the conduct of the war. It does not seem, however, that Chamberlain himself made any important contribution to his knowledge.

'It does not seem' is an important qualification. What actually takes place at the monarch's weekly meeting with the prime minister is one of the most jealously guarded secrets in political Britain. Marcia Falkender, Harold Wilson's most intimate associate, remarked that Wilson had only once divulged to her what had been discussed at the Palace – and that was when the subject had been the style of riding habit the queen was to wear for the ceremony of Trooping the Colour. While Chamberlain was prime minister the silence was total. All the evidence suggests, however, that while the king admired and respected Chamberlain and felt that he was the right man for the job, there was little real warmth between them. The king never found personal communication easy, Chamberlain was by nature cool and withdrawn; the two minds may have met, but the meeting can never have achieved anything approaching intimacy.

George VI had hoped that, once war began, Chamberlain would form a government of national unity, including both Labour and Liberal ministers. Chamberlain was not minded to do anything of the sort; his greatest concession to the wartime spirit was to take back those dissident Conservatives, Churchill and Eden, into the Cabinet. Ironically, in the light of later developments, it was those same two ministers whom the king found it most difficult to like or trust. 'I find he [Eden] does not give me confidence,' he wrote in his diary. 'Winston is difficult to talk to, but in time I shall get the right technique, I hope.'[1] He also had his doubts about the Secretary of State for War, Leslie Hore-Belisha. Hore-Belisha was efficient, far-sighted and imaginative and had done much to refurbish some of the more antiquated features of the British army; he was also querulous, quarrelsome and conspicuously short of charm. One of the most bitter of his quarrels was with Lord Gort, the Chief of the Imperial General Staff. A situation in which the minister responsible for the army is virtually not on speaking terms with the senior soldier is obviously untenable at any time, particularly in time of war. The king knew both men well and was privately convinced that, if one had to go, it should be Belisha. How far, if at all, he allowed this view to become known to the prime minister is uncertain. Belisha for one was convinced that the king was agitating for his removal but it seems more likely that he did no more than pass on to Chamberlain the views that Gort had expressed to him in the course of a royal visit to the British troops in France. Typically, Chamberlain did not get round to telling the king that he was trying to persuade Belisha to switch to another office within the government – the war minister's sudden resignation came as a complete surprise.

So long as the war grumbled along with nothing much happening, Chamberlain could remain safely in No.10, backed by the greater part of the enormous Conservative majority in the House of Commons. The disastrous campaign in Norway in April 1940 imperilled his position; when the Germans overran the Low Countries and the

Labour Party refused to join a national government under his leadership, even he accepted that he had to go. George VI still hoped that the Labour leader, Clement Attlee, could be persuaded to change his mind and join a coalition under Chamberlain. He offered to intervene to try to bring this about: 'I said that I felt what I call the great triumvirate, the PM, Halifax and Winston, could not be bettered.'[2] The offer was not accepted: the timing was not right, Chamberlain considered. Almost certainly it would have made no difference; Labour were resolved that Chamberlain must go. The king had to accept the inevitable. He did so with reluctance. On 17 May the queen wrote a personal letter to Chamberlain to express their sorrow: 'I can never tell you in words how much we owe you. During these last desperate and unhappy years, you have been a great support and comfort to us both, and we felt so safe with the knowledge that your wisdom and high purpose were there at our hand.'[3] The words were those of the queen but they reflected faithfully the feelings of her husband.

If Chamberlain had to go, then George VI had no doubt that the foreign secretary, Lord Halifax, would be the best man to replace him. Halifax was an old and trusted friend; he was a safe man, prudent, predictable; he spoke the same sort of language as the king. The only realistic alternative was Churchill; the king recognized his merits and accepted that he should remain at the Admiralty but was nervous about his potentiality as a national leader. Churchill was a maverick, adventurous, unsound. The king could not wholly put out of his mind the fact that he had been a prominent champion of Edward VIII at the time of the abdication, nor that he had been the most conspicuous opponent of Chamberlain over appeasement. But Halifax, when approached, refused to be considered for the job, pleading that in contemporary Britain, especially in wartime, the prime minister must be in the House of Commons. The king suggested that Halifax's peerage might be put in abeyance for the duration of the war. Halifax would not contemplate the idea; he knew that he could not command the support he would need in the House of Commons and was wise enough to recognize that he did not possess the qualities needed for a wartime leader. Like it or not, it was inevitable that George VI's next prime minister should be Winston Churchill. 'I cannot yet think of Winston as PM,' he wrote in his diary. 'I met Halifax in the garden and I told him I was sorry not to have him as PM.'[4]

The relationship got off to a frosty start. Though the king said nothing to Churchill to suggest that he was unhappy about the appointment, the new prime minister can hardly have been unaware that he was not altogether welcome. An early source of disagreement was Churchill's inclusion in his government of his old crony, the powerful and somewhat disreputable Canadian press magnate, Lord Beaverbrook. George VI was horrified: in a handwritten letter he urged Churchill to reconsider his decision, which the king, rather obscurely, suggested might be 'misconstrued'. 'You are no doubt aware that the Canadians do not appreciate him,' he wrote; and since Canada played a vital role in the training of pilots for the RAF, it seemed injudicious to thrust Beaverbrook upon them.[5] He took equally strong exception to the appointment as privy councillor of the still more raffish

Brendan Bracken – alleged by some, on shaky grounds, to be Churchill's illegitimate son. In neither case did the prime minister pay much attention to his monarch's susceptibilities; and when he compounded his sins by consistently being late for his audiences at the Palace, the king felt he had every reason to hanker for the more amenable services of Lord Halifax.

It did not last. Churchill – though accommodating the whims of the Palace might seem to come low in his list of priorities – was at heart a devoted monarchist. He quickly came to respect the common sense and balanced judgement of the king. George VI for his part realized that Churchill was indispensable as wartime leader and in time derived great pleasure from his meetings with that ebullient and immensely stimulating statesman. The formal audiences were replaced by casual lunches at which the two talked freely without any servants being present: 'I could not have a better Prime Minister,' the king wrote in his diary a few months after Churchill came to power.[6]

The king, too, rejoiced in the fact that at last he had a truly national government. Though he genuinely welcomed the advent of the Labour ministers, he was nevertheless at first somewhat apprehensive. Until the formation of the Coalition government in 1940 he had seen little of them; they were civil enough when met casually but he suspected that revolutionary tendencies might lurk beneath the surface. Getting to know them in wartime quickly disabused him. Nobody could have seemed less like a revolutionary than Clement Attlee; the king found him difficult to communicate with but then so did everyone else, whatever their political allegiance. It was one of the miracles of the age that a man so profoundly uncommunicative should have got to the top of a profession in which to be articulate is generally felt to be a first essential. Ernest Bevin was another matter. George VI enormously appreciated his frankness, good sense and earthy humour. Nor did Herbert Morrison seem threatening; he was less attractive a personality than Bevin but quite as far removed from being an anti-monarchist. Hugh Dalton the king disliked, but then everyone disliked Dalton, not for his political views but because he was so eminently dislikeable. The fact that George VI got to know and trust the socialist members of the coalition was to make things immeasurably easier when he found himself confronted by a Labour government in 1945.

Keeping abreast of the course of the war was important, but did not solve the question posed at the beginning of this chapter: what was a king supposed to do in wartime? He broadcast to the nation on the evening after war was declared and was generally felt to have provided a rallying call of singular potency, but he could not repeat this feat with any regularity. Many of the traditional public appearances of the king were suspended for the duration. He visited the troops and took every chance he could to boost morale and preach the virtues of the Allied cause, but he was underemployed and acutely conscious of the fact.

Everything changed in the autumn of 1940. As the German army surged across Europe and invasion seemed imminent, the king installed shooting ranges at Buckingham Palace and Windsor where he and the queen honed their skills with pistols and tommy guns so as to confront the Germans if they came. There was talk of sending the two princesses to Canada, but the idea was postponed indefinitely; as for the king, if his country were occupied, it was his intention either to die in its defence or, if he was spared, to join the resistance movement and continue the fight. Then began the Blitz on Britain's cities. The king and queen were indefatigable in touring the districts that had been bombed, picking their way through the debris, visiting people in their shattered homes, condoling, sympathizing, enquiring. It made not the slightest difference to the physical plight of the victims, but the knowledge that they were not forgotten, that the king and queen knew what was going on and wanted to share their misery, made an immeasurable difference to their morale.

In London the German bombers at first concentrated their attacks on the docks and the East End. A suspicion grew that this was a poor man's war, that there was some tacit understanding between the leaders on both sides that as far as possible the more affluent areas should be spared. Fortunately for the spirit of national unity the Germans extended their attacks to the West End; more fortunately still, they made Buckingham Palace a target. Twice the Palace was hit, once by a lone bomber which some believed was piloted by the king's cousin, Prince Christopher of Hesse. Neither the king nor the queen was injured, but they were within thirty yards of the second bomb and the windows of the royal apartments were blown in. 'I'm glad we've been bombed,' the queen famously remarked. 'It makes me feel I can look the East End in the face.'[7]

In all the palaces, austerity was the order of the day.

Every bath had a black line painted on its side to indicate that there should never be more than five inches of water; food and drink were sternly limited – dismayingly so in the eyes of certain visitors, who had hoped that in the Palace at least they might get a decent meal; central heating was eschewed; there should never be more than one light in a bedroom. There was an element of play-acting in this – inevitably the king was better fed and more comfortably housed than the majority of his subjects – but the privations were real and the king's wish that he should share the sufferings of his subjects was totally sincere.

Like so many of his people, the king also endured the loss of a member of his family. In August 1942 his brother, the Duke of Kent, was killed when the plane in which he was travelling to visit RAF establishments in Iceland crashed in the Scottish mountains. The king had never been particularly close to his brother, who by tastes and temperament was nearer to the Duke of Windsor, but he had got to know him better in the last few years and was shocked by his sudden death. The funeral was at St George's, Windsor. 'I have attended very many family funerals in the Chapel,' wrote the king in his diary, 'but none which has moved me in the same way.'[8]

'I wish I had a definite job like you,' the king had written wistfully to Mountbatten shortly after the outbreak of war.[9] By 1942 he still had no 'definite job' but he had made a place for himself and was taken seriously by Churchill and the other ministers. One innovation for which he was personally responsible was the George Cross. He refused to accept the traditional view that civilians could not be fighting 'in the face of the enemy' and were therefore by definition ineligible for any award for gallantry. This might have been true in earlier wars, but how could it still be the case when the Blitz had brought death and destruction to so many British cities? The George Cross and the George Medal were his answer: he not only conceived the idea but was largely responsible for the design of the decorations themselves. Still more imaginative was his suggestion that a George Cross should be awarded collectively to the people of Malta, the Mediterranean island which had endured many months of bombardment and almost unbearable privations. Against the advice of his more cautious counsellors, he insisted on visiting the island himself in June 1942 in the course of a tour he was making of the Allied forces in North Africa. As with his visits to Blitzed cities, his arrival in no way mitigated the plight of the Maltese but it convinced them that their sufferings were known about and appreciated. In the Middle Ages it was believed that the royal touch could cure certain unpleasant diseases. Few would have credited it with such potency in the twentieth century, but the royal presence still had near-magical properties to raise the spirits and enhance the self-respect of those who had been left sorely battered by the war.

The king's personal relationship with President Roosevelt, though almost as imponderable as his effect on the morale of the people of Malta, was seen by the government as a potent asset, to be used with restraint but to good effect. When a somewhat reluctant Halifax was packed off on the battleship *King George V* to serve as British ambassador in Washington, the president personally went to welcome him.

George VI wrote to thank him; it was, he said, 'a gesture which I and my countrymen deeply appreciated'.[10] The gesture was quickly reciprocated: when the new American ambassador, J. G. Winant, paid his call at Windsor Castle, the king went to the railway station to meet him. It was the first time that a British monarch had ever gone out to meet a foreign ambassador; 'and I didn't even have a battleship,' wrote Winant wonderingly.[11] The gesture was followed up: the king took particular pains to cultivate his friendship with Winant and with the president's personal envoy, Henry Hopkins. Good republicans and hard-boiled politicians as both men were, they were not likely to be seduced by royal amiability; but it is obvious from their reports that they appreciated the effort and found the king unexpectedly well informed, sensible and easy to talk to.

Meanwhile the king's relationship with his prime minister became ever closer. The initial differences of opinion over Beaverbrook and Brendan Bracken were quickly forgotten, increasingly Churchill consulted George VI about new appointments and on one occasion at least – involving the choice of Lord Cranborne as Dominions Secretary – changed his mind as a result of persuasion from the Palace. The king for his part accepted that this titanic figure in Downing Street was the best, even the only, man to control Britain's destinies and that the role of the Palace must be to support him. He did not, however, assume Churchill to be immune from criticism. 'I do not feel at all happy about the present political situation in North Africa,' he wrote sharply in February 1943.[12] He went on to list his doubts and concluded with his need for 'an assurance from you that they are being carefully watched'. He got it; Churchill replied with a long and thoughtful memorandum which admitted the force of the king's misgivings and explained what was being done to counter them. The popular image is of a weak and somewhat ineffective king rubber-stamping the decisions of his dictatorial minister. The reality is more nuanced and more interesting. Churchill was obviously the dominant force in the partnership, but it *was* a partnership, and the king's role in it was far from negligible.

George VI's most significant duty was to be a figurehead, a rallying point which embodied the pride and determination of his country. The problem about this was that Churchill – through his pugnacity, his eloquence, his splendid presence – to some extent usurped the king's role. *He* was the focal point: the symbol of Britain's will to resist to the last man, whatever the odds against it. He would have been dismayed if he had been told that he was thus putting his monarch in the shade; nor did the king, even in the privacy of his diary, ever protest that he was being allotted too small a role. George VI was only human, though; it is hard to believe that he never resented the fact that it was Churchill, Churchill, Churchill all the way while the head of state was left to play a secondary role.

On at least one occasion the king confronted his prime minister and won the day. It related to D-Day, the operation that launched the Second Front in June 1944. Both men conceived the idea that they should take part in the battle, travelling with the immense armada that was to cross the Channel. Without too much difficulty the king was persuaded that this would be a futile enterprise: he would see

very little and, more important, by his presence and the need
to secure his safety he would distract people who ought to
be totally concentrated on their great enterprise. Churchill
proved more obstinate. He agreed that the king's presence
would be undesirable but insisted that he would nevertheless go himself. 'I am very worried over the PM's seemingly
selfish way of looking at the matter,' the king wrote in his
diary.[13] He brooded over the business for another night and
then sent Churchill a further letter. He was a younger man
than Churchill, he pointed out, a sailor, and 'as King head
of all three Services. There is nothing I would like better
than to go to sea but I have agreed to stop at home; is it fair
that you should then do exactly what I should have liked to
do myself?' Possibly Churchill had already begun to weaken
in his resolve; grumblingly he gave way. 'Since Your Majesty does me the honour to be so much concerned about my
personal safety,' he wrote, 'I must defer to Your Majesty's
wishes and indeed commands.' There was nobody else
whose commands Churchill would have heeded; for the
sake of amicable relations between the Palace and No.10 it
was probably lucky that the king did not think it necessary
to utter such commands on other occasions.

George VI mourned the loss of his younger brother; his
elder brother he could well have done without. When war
broke out he offered to send a plane to the South of France
to collect the Windsors; some unspecified job would then
be found for the duke so that he could at least appear to
be serving his country. The duke found the offer unappeal-
ing and refused it, then thought better of his decision and

begged the use of a destroyer to return to England. Any hopes he had that there would be a real reconciliation and that his wife would be received at court were quickly extinguished. Neither the queen nor Queen Mary had any intention of meeting the woman whom the queen still rather uncivilly referred to as 'Mrs S'. After a few days the duke called on his brother at Buckingham Palace; conveniently, the queen was out of London so no women were included in the meeting.

Remarkably, the king seemed still to labour under the illusion that his brother was a potent force who would gather much popular support if he remained in Britain. To Hore-Belisha he remarked regretfully that all his ancestors had succeeded to the throne after their predecessors had died, but 'Mine is not only alive, but very much so.'[14] The duke was packed off to France, to serve on a military mission under the command of Major-General Howard Vyse. No one seemed very sure what the mission was supposed to be doing, still less what part in its activities the duke was intended to play. In fact he made himself modestly useful and wrote some quite perceptive reports on the state of the French units which he visited. He quickly concluded, however, that he was wasting his time and that the ruling that he should not be allowed to visit British units not merely made his job impossible but was deliberately insulting. 'Maybe you hate me and always have,' he told the king. 'You have certainly disguised it very well in the past, especially when I was King.'[15]

Things changed in May 1940 when the Germans broke through the French lines and put the Allies to rout. Having had little to do before, he now had nothing; he conducted a personal retreat and ended up in Spain. His behaviour up to that point had been, if not commendable, then at least possible to justify; when he now refused to return to Britain without a guarantee that he and his wife would be received at court he had unequivocally gone too far. The king was outraged and at first was inclined to let his brother sink or swim by himself. In the end Churchill suggested that the duke should be made Governor of the Bahamas. He must have some sort of job, the king conceded, 'and though there may be criticism and the Bahamian ladies won't like it,'[16] it was at least better than having him at home. It was October 1945 before the two brothers met again.

By that time the Japanese had surrendered and the war was over. The king could congratulate himself on having had what could fairly be called 'a good war'. He had done everything that had been asked of him and more besides. He had travelled widely, and though his face might not have been the most famous in the country it was known by almost everyone. His broadcasts had moved the nation, not by their eloquence but by the patent sincerity and deep feeling which permeated every sentence. Far more of his subjects than had ever been the case before knew the king and queen, not just as distant images but as live human beings. With the continent in chaos and communism rampant and threatening to take over in France and Italy, it was critically important that there should be political stability in Britain. It was not just thanks to the king that such stability existed, but if the monarchy had been unpopular, if there had been a republican movement of any significance, the task of those who battled to keep Britain on an even keel would have been immeasurably harder.

In wartime it had been evident what everyone had to do; there might be terrible perils to overcome but the path of duty was clearly signposted. With peace the king accepted there would be new and more complicated problems. He would have been superhuman – or plain foolish – if he had not felt apprehensive about the future. In the meantime, though, there was a moment for rejoicing. As always at the climactic moments of modern British history, huge crowds assembled in front of Buckingham Palace, calling for the king. Eight times the king and queen appeared on the balcony to vast applause; they could have done the same eighty times without any abatement of the enthusiasm. Under the escort of a few young Guards officers Princess Elizabeth and Princess Margaret were allowed to venture out to mix with the exultant crowds. 'Poor darlings, they have never had any fun yet,' was the king's final entry in his wartime diary.

6
The Final Years

Even before the war against Japan had ended the king found himself confronted by an earthquake in domestic politics. The coalition had broken up after the German surrender and Churchill had decided that it would be better to hold an immediate election rather than to cling on for a little longer. He was the hero who was seen to have won the war, but there was another war still to be won; most people took it for granted that he would be returned with a large majority. The king was not so certain. His private opinion was that no party would have an overall majority. The most likely prospect was that the Conservatives would emerge as the largest party and would form a coalition with the Liberals. That Churchill would remain prime minister he took for granted – a view that was probably shared by the Labour leader, Clement Attlee.

Instead, Labour emerged from the election with a massive majority. The result was freakish: in terms of popular votes Labour was the largest party but substantially smaller than the Conservatives and Liberals combined; in parliamentary seats it had a huge overall majority. Churchill was out. 'I think that Bertie felt it very much,' the queen told Queen Mary. 'Winston has been such a great support and comfort through these terrible years.'[1] George VI's reaction provided a curious echo of his response when Chamberlain had given way to Churchill in 1940. 'I was shocked at the result,' he told his outgoing prime minister, 'and I thought it most ungrateful to you personally after all your hard work for the people.'[2]

He knew quite well, however, that he could not allow such feelings to colour his attitude towards his new ministers. Privately, he was dismayed by the thought of the policies which a socialist government was bound to introduce. His conservative instincts had grown, if anything, more pronounced with the years. If a Tory government had been returned he would certainly have urged them to adopt liberal policies, but he viewed the prospect of a lurch to the left with alarm and distaste. To some extent he was comforted by his personal knowledge of the new ministers. Attlee in particular he knew and trusted. As Churchill's deputy prime minister during the war Attlee had frequently visited Buckingham Palace and he had won the king's confidence, if not his affection. Perhaps even more important, Attlee had learned to respect and admire the king; George VI was sure that he could speak freely to his new prime minister and that he would be listened to. When Attlee proposed that Hugh Dalton should be foreign secretary the king did not hesitate to demur and to suggest that Ernest Bevin would serve much better in that role. It is indicative of Attlee's high opinion of George VI, both as a monarch and as a sound judge of character, that he took this advice and appointed Dalton Chancellor of the Exchequer.

But the king's respect for his new prime minister did not

translate into any kind of intimacy. Attlee in his new role was no more communicative than he had been during the war; the weekly audience, which had been such a delight when Churchill had been the other protagonist, became an ordeal to be looked forward to with resignation if not dismay. Even if Attlee had been all that was most companionable, however, the king would have been distressed by much of what he said. George VI privately deplored most of the new government's legislation. He felt that he could not protest at his ministers carrying out the mandate that they had clearly been given by the electorate; what he did openly complain about, though, was the pace at which things were done. A torrent of legislation was unleashed in the first years of the Labour government, including the nationalization of coal-mining, gas, electricity, road and rail transport, the infrastructure on which a modern state was based. With a National Health Service thrown in for good measure, it seemed to the king that almost nothing was being left of the world in which he had been brought up.

He urged restraint: not suggesting that the government should take a different course but that it should proceed more cautiously in the same direction. What alarmed him most was that he felt the role of the state was being made ever more invasive and that of the individual less significant. In his diary he recorded that he had told Attlee 'that he must give the people here some confidence that the government was not going to stifle all private enterprise. Everyone wanted to help in rehabilitating the country but they were not allowed to.'³ He became still more alarmed when, in August 1947, the opposition denounced the government for introducing legislation which, it was claimed, would give it something close to totalitarian powers. It does not seem likely that Churchill really believed Attlee to be a would-be dictator, but it was a convenient stick with which to beat the Labour government and he wielded it with great relish. The king took it seriously – more seriously than it deserved – and wrote anxiously to Attlee offering, or perhaps threatening, to return to London from Balmoral if a serious constitutional crisis was in the offing. Attlee did not have too much difficulty in convincing the king that the democratic system was not in peril, but the fact that George VI had harboured any such doubts showed that his mind was never going to be entirely at ease while a government dedicated to radical reform remained in power.

Crippling economic problems were exacerbated by the Americans abruptly cutting off Lend-Lease, damaging strikes, shortages of food, oil and coal, a series of viciously intemperate winters: Britain was in a mess. 'I have asked Mr Attlee 3 times now if he is not worried over the domestic situation in this country,' the king wrote in his diary in January 1947. 'But he won't tell me he is when I feel he is. I know *I* am worried.'[4] Given his remarkably phlegmatic disposition it is possible that Attlee really was not worried, but, if so, he must have been one of the few people in the country to feel so sanguine.

A month later George VI was able to escape, if not his main concerns, then at least their constant physical presence around him. With the queen and the two princesses he set out on the battleship HMS *Vanguard* on the way to South Africa. He knew that the visit was not going to

1. Prince Albert in the sailor suit which he fondly believed would be his uniform throughout his working life

2. The official engagement photograph of the Duke of York and Lady Elizabeth Bowes-Lyon

3. The Prince of Wales and the Duke of York out with the Belvoir Hunt

4. Wimbledon 1923, partnered by Louis Greig

5. At Glamis in 1927 with the inevitable dogs

6. The Duke and Duchess of York at Sandwich in 1931 with Princess Elizabeth and an infant Princess Margaret Rose

7. The King with General Eisenhower in North Africa in June 1943

8. The King visiting Malta in June 1943; it was his idea that a George Cross should be collectively awarded to the people of Malta

9. King George VI with President Roosevelt in Washington in 1939

10. The King with Winston Churchill, 8 May 1945

11. One of the last photographs of the King, taken in late
November 1951

be a rest cure and it was bound to involve some tricky political manoeuvring. Field Marshal Smuts, the South African prime minister, was an ardent supporter of Great Britain and the empire and had done more than anyone to ensure that South Africa had supported the Allies loyally during the recent war. A general election was pending and a tacit purpose of the royal visit was to try to contribute to Smuts' chances of victory. But a larger proportion of the white population was Afrikaans-speaking and of this group the majority had little use for the empire, still less for its titular monarch. George VI saw his role as being to court their favour and to contrive that, even if they could not be persuaded to vote for Smuts, they would at least be content to remain part of the British Empire. Left to himself, the king would also have consorted freely with what was by far the most numerous section of the population: the Africans, Indians and Coloureds. The full horror of *apartheid* still lay in the future, but even under Smuts the black man was very much a second-class citizen. The king was distressed by the fact that, when he greeted a white veteran of the Second World War, he was expected to shake him by the hand, whereas if the soldier was black any such physical contact was considered demeaning. He was tempted to ignore the rule and to treat black and white alike, but he remembered why he was in South Africa. Gratuitously to offend a large section of the white population would achieve the opposite results to those he hoped for.

For the king the visit to South Africa was doubly significant because he was accompanied not only by his wife but by his two daughters. The projection of 'the royal family' as a united and loving unit may have seemed to some of his advisers principally a useful propaganda device, but to the king it was a cherished reality. He remembered how little time his own parents had been able to devote to their children and was resolved that he would not make the same mistake. The concept of 'the family firm' was all-important to him. It was in South Africa that Princess Elizabeth came of age and, in a moving broadcast, dedicated herself to the service of her future subjects in Great Britain, the Commonwealth and the empire. The next generation pledged itself to carry on the work of the present rulers; she can have had no idea how soon that burden was going to fall on her.

Even by the time she made that promise, the king's ideal of 'the family firm' as an exclusive and closely knit unit had been questioned. Ever since she had first seen him at Dartmouth in 1943, Princess Elizabeth had known that she wanted to marry her cousin, Prince Philip of Greece. The king played for time – she was too young to make up her mind, Philip must be given an opportunity to establish himself in his career – but the young couple stuck to their guns and, by the time of the South African tour, it had been accepted that their eventual marriage was inevitable. There were problems, though. Prince Philip had no money and no name – Schleswig-Holstein-Sonderburg-Glücksburg was as near as one could get, and that hardly seemed appropriate for the husband of a future British monarch. Virtually, he had no nationality – the Greek royal family was German in origin and had only the most precarious standing in the country over which it was supposed to rule, while Philip himself had spent almost all his life in Britain. The money didn't matter – there was plenty of that on the other side; his mother's name, 'Mountbatten', seemed entirely acceptable; Prince Philip was eager to take on British citizenship. The difficulties melted away. The important things were that the prince was clearly an estimable character and that the king liked him. The engagement was announced shortly after the royal family returned to Britain.

Britain was still short of food and fuel; clothing was old and shabby; the ravages of war were evident in every way. The temptation must have been to make the wedding a low-key affair, to avoid any accusations that the royal family was celebrating lavishly while the people starved. Instead, with the enthusiastic support of the government, they decided that this was an occasion for rejoicing; the nation needed to be cheered up. A colourful wedding with all the accoutrements of carriages, cavalry escort and a splendid wedding dress created by Norman Hartnell seemed well suited for the purpose. Compared with some of the jollifications over the next sixty years the affair was notably modest, but at the time it seemed extraordinary. The gamble, if it was a gamble, paid off handsomely. Huge crowds watched the procession, many millions more followed the ceremony on the wireless. What little criticism there was was muted; the British people revelled in the opportunity to show that they liked the monarchy and took much pleasure in an event that seemed to guarantee its prolonged existence.

Princess Margaret was still a teenager when her sister married. She was pretty, lively, impatient, irreverent and headstrong: a combination which seemed likely to cause problems in the future. Her father greatly complicated the course of her life when he took on as an equerry the handsome, dashing and much-decorated fighter pilot Peter Townsend. Townsend made himself extremely popular and, when his marriage broke up, he was allowed to stay on, contrary to the normal rule of the time that divorced people were not acceptable at court. The romance with Princess Margaret followed, though it did not become public until well after the king's death. 'I have really felt quite shattered by the whole thing,' wrote the – by then – Queen Mother, 'and cannot help feeling that it would never have happened if the king had been here.'[5] Her faith in her husband's paternal authority was touching, but it seems more likely that he would have been as blind as she was to what was happening. Whether he would have handled matters differently is impossible to say. The new queen let Churchill make the running and accepted his ruling that Princess Margaret could only marry Townsend if she renounced all her royal rights and privileges. Perhaps the king would have been more inclined to put his younger daughter's happiness before the traditional proprieties. In any case, it would have caused him much worry; his premature death saved him from one painful headache at least.

'I have not', Winston Churchill had defiantly declared in 1942, 'become the King's First Minister in order to preside over the liquidation of the British Empire.'[6] When it came to the point he couldn't do much about it, though – any more than could the king whose first minister he was. The dramatically rapid disintegration of King George's empire for the most part took place in the reign of his daughter, but the writing was on the wall long before he died. It was the granting of independence to India in 1947 that made inevitable all that followed. Given Churchill's denunciation of the Labour government's surrender to what he held to be the demands of an irresponsible and unrepresentative minority, it is surprising to find that as early as July 1942 he had told the king that it was inevitable that independence would have to be ceded after the war was over. George VI was alarmed and distressed by this opinion: 'India has got to be governed, and this will have to be our policy,' he told Churchill.[7] It wasn't the Labour government's policy; no more than the king did Attlee believe India was ready for self-government, but he knew that Britain did not have the resources to retain the subcontinent by force, especially in the face of American opposition. Now it was Churchill who, freed from the responsibilities of office, indulged himself in denouncing what he described as an ignoble scuttle. The king, on the other hand, as ever pragmatic and reasonable, accepted the inevitable and made no effort to dissuade his prime minister. Indeed, he became directly involved when Attlee proposed to appoint the former Supreme Commander in South East Asia as the last viceroy. Mountbatten had no wish to take on the job; if his cousin the king had shown any doubts about the wisdom of the appointment he would gratefully have refused it. The king did not. He was prepared to make fun of Mountbatten's vanity and egotism, but he greatly admired his clear-headed dynamism and powers both to persuade and to lead. He thought his cousin was the best man for the task and urged him to accept it. If he had done otherwise then the fate of British India might have been very different.

The former Emperor of India accepted the loss of his role with resignation. In this as in so many things, he knew that his government was doing no more than what it had been elected to do. As king he saw his role as being to support them, certainly to offer no overt opposition. But he could not pretend always to be happy at what was going on. When he was awarding an honour to the writer Vita Sackville-West, he asked her what was happening to her ancestral home, Knole. It had been taken over by the National Trust, she said. The king threw up his hands in dismay. 'Everything is going, nowadays,' he said. 'Before long I shall also have to go.'[8]

In the case of India he comforted himself with the reflection that the three new nations – India, Pakistan and what is now Sri Lanka – had all opted to join the British Commonwealth. This posed an immediate problem, however. George VI was King of Australia, King of Canada, King, therefore, of the Commonwealth, but India in particular was resolved to be a republic. The proposed solution was to style him not King but Head of the Commonwealth. If he had been disposed to make difficulties, to stand on his dignity, it is conceivable that the whole enterprise might have foundered. He believed, however, that an extended Commonwealth, to which all or nearly all the former colonial countries would belong, might be a powerful force for good in the world. This he held to be far more important that any question of what title he should bear. The process was not completed before his death, George VI was never Head of the Commonwealth, but the principle had been accepted, the extended Commonwealth was a reality.

By that time he had a new prime minister – or rather, had reverted to the previous one. When Attlee went to the country in February 1950 both he and the king thought it probable that Labour would be returned with a reduced but still substantial majority. Instead there was a dramatic swing to the right. At one moment it seemed as if Labour was going to lose its overall majority. The king had found that he could live quite happily with a Labour government, he would have been pleased if a strong Conservative government had taken its place; the thing he most feared was an equivocal result which would provoke a constitutional crisis. In such a case he would have to take some decisive action, at the risk of offending one party and with the possibility of offending both. 'Yesterday was one of the worst days of my life wondering what was going to happen,' he recorded.[9] In the event Labour was left with a tiny overall majority. The king's fear was then that Attlee might ask for an immediate dissolution and a fresh election. Theoretically the king would have been within his rights to refuse the request, in which case Attlee would certainly have resigned; if he had done as Attlee wanted, however, it seemed more than possible that the stalemate would have been repeated and the political crisis continued with still greater acrimony. To his unconcealed relief Attlee decided that he would soldier on till he was defeated in the House of Commons. In the event the government lasted for another eighteen months.

Unusually, the king played some part in deciding the date of the next election; he was due to embark on a lengthy tour of Australia and New Zealand and told his prime minister that he would not feel able to leave the country while the political situation seemed so unstable. Attlee responded by calling an election in October 1951. The king braced himself for a repeat of 1950, with the two parties evenly balanced, but to his relief the Conservatives won an overall majority of nearly twenty. It was not as much as they would have liked, but it was enough. Churchill was back. The king sent for him with undisguised satisfaction, but he quickly showed that he had lost none of his determination to protect his royal rights. Churchill proposed that Anthony Eden, once more foreign secretary, should also carry the title of deputy prime minister. This would not have been the first time that the title had been used but the king felt it was a dangerous practice, suggesting that Eden would succeed Churchill automatically and that the king's right to send for the prime minister of his choice would be weakened, if not abolished. Churchill accepted the ruling without demur. It was still generally assumed that Eden would succeed Churchill, but the decision whether or not to offer him the post remained the king's. The royal prerogative had been preserved.

By then the king was already a dying man. By the end of the war he was physically and mentally exhausted. 'I feel burned out,' was his constant refrain. He never fully recovered; the South African expedition, though in some ways a welcome escape, had proved exceptionally demanding and by 1948 he was beginning to experience attacks of cramp in both legs. His doctors were sufficiently alarmed to recommend that the visit to Australia and New Zealand, which was planned for the spring of 1949, should be postponed. Privately, they suspected that it would be more a case of abandonment than deferral. It seemed unlikely that he would ever again be well enough to undertake so strenuous a journey: arteriosclerosis had been the diagnosis, with the possibility of gangrene. The king was most reluctant to accept the doctors' verdict: he believed that he was pledged to visit the dominions, that millions of people would be disappointed if he did not do so and that it was therefore his duty to make the trip, painful though it might be. In the end, however, he gave way. That, he assumed, would be the end of the matter; he was indignant and upset when he was told that, in spite of his having truckled to his doctors, his condition had so far deteriorated that a major operation was necessary. It took place in March 1949 and seemed to have been successful. The king began to pick up the threads of his official life again: he accepted, though reluctantly, that there were limits to the number of things he could do without taxing his strength too far; he even cut down on the disastrously heavy smoking which must have been an important factor in his illness. The doctors knew that he was never going to be an entirely fit man again but they rejoiced in his improvement and believed, or at least professed to believe, that there was no reason why he should not keep going for another ten or twenty years. They even suggested that, by 1952, he might be fit enough to undertake the long-postponed visit to Australia.

They proved too optimistic. The summer of 1951 saw him struck down by influenza, which clung on and threatened to develop into pneumonia. His doctors became ever more alarmed, and by September recommended an exploratory operation. Privately they must have suspected what the result was likely to be: the king had lung cancer, and an immediate operation to remove the diseased lung was essential. It seems that the king was never given the full facts about his condition; he took an informed interest in his health, however, and may have suspected the truth. It was perhaps one of those occasions on which somebody prefers not to ask a question because he thinks he will not like the answer, but George VI was unflinching in his readiness to confront the truth and it seems more likely that he genuinely did not realize how ill he was.

By the time the election of 1951 restored Churchill to Downing Street the king, superficially at least, seemed to be once more on the way to recovery. His plan was to visit South Africa in March 1952, this time not to undertake a strenuous tour but to recuperate in the house which the government had put at his disposal. In the meantime he despatched his daughter and Prince Philip on the tour of Australia and New Zealand which he had finally accepted he could not undertake himself. That done, he returned to Sandringham. February 5 was a dry, cold, sunny day, perfect for the kind of informal shoot which he most enjoyed. Tired but contented, he retired to bed. He never woke. When his valet brought him his tea at 7.30 the following morning he found that the king was dead.

*

King George V had returned to Buckingham Palace after driving round the East End as part of the celebration of his Silver Jubilee in 1935. Immense crowds had cheered him along the way. 'I'd no idea they felt like that about me,' he remarked with tears in his eyes. If George VI had been in a position to watch what was happening in London after his death he might have said something very similar. Hundreds of thousands of his subjects showed their feelings by queuing for up to twelve hours in the rain and snow to file past his coffin in Westminster Hall. A curious observer asked one of the queuers why he was putting himself to such discomfort. 'Well, it's the King, ain't it?' was the reply. 'Wouldn't do it for anyone else, mind you.' 'He's *my* King and I want to say goodbye to him,' said another mourner.[10] Vast crowds lined the streets for the funeral, smaller than for the coronation some fifteen years before when there had been large stands and many months of preparation, but far larger than any non-royal occasion could have assembled. 'He's my King' would have been the instinctive response of almost everyone who had patiently waited for several hours to see the cortège go by.

George VI lacked almost all the qualities that go to make popular heroes. He was not glamorous, not eloquent, in no way dashing. He was high-principled, sober, loyal, reliable, honourable, extraordinary in his ordinariness. He was George the Dutiful. He was a good king; more important than that, he was a good man. It was thanks to him that Queen Elizabeth II inherited a throne as secure as any in the world.

Notes

1. YOUTH

1. Michael Bloch, *The Secret File of the Duke of Windsor* (London: Bantam, 1988), p. 277.
2. Philip Ziegler, *King Edward VIII* (London: Collins, 1990), p. 79.
3. Harold Nicolson, *King George V: His Life and Reign* (London: Constable, 1952), p. 51.
4. Sarah Bradford, *George VI* (London: Weidenfeld & Nicolson, 1989), p. 45.

2. DUKE OF YORK

1. Ziegler, *Edward VIII*, p. 49.
2. Ibid., p. 64.
3. Bradford, *George VI*, p. 109.
4. John Wheeler-Bennett, *King George VI* (London: Macmillan, 1958), p. 126.
5. Ibid., p. 131.
6. *The Times*, 21/4/17.
7. Ibid., 2/2/52.
8. Wheeler-Bennett, *George VI*, p. 140.
9. William Shawcross, *Queen Elizabeth: The Queen Mother* (London: Macmillan, 2009), p. 37.
10. Wheeler-Bennett, *George VI*, p. 213.
11. Private information.

3. ABDICATION

1. William Teeling, *Corridors of Frustration* (London: Johnson, 1970), p. 104.
2. Wheeler-Bennett, *George VI*, p. 23.
3. *Counting One's Blessings: The Selected Letters of Queen Elizabeth the Queen Mother*, ed. William Shawcross (London: Macmillan, 2012), p. 221.
4. Wheeler-Bennett, *George VI*, pp. 282–3.
5. *Counting One's Blessings*, p. 226.
6. Bradford, *George VI*, p. 180.
7. Wheeler-Bennett, *George VI*, p. 286.

8. Ibid., p. 283.
9. 'Chips': The Diaries of Sir Henry Channon, ed. Robert Rhodes-James (London: Weidenfeld & Nicolson, 1967), p. 100.
10. Philip Ziegler, Mountbatten (London: 2001), p. 95.

4. BECOMING THE KING

1. Robert Rhodes-James, A Spirit Undaunted: The Political Role of George VI (London: Little, Brown, 1998), p. 115.
2. Harold Nicolson, Diaries and Letters 1930–39, ed. Nigel Nicolson (London: Collins, 1966), p. 115.
3. Ziegler, Edward VIII, p. 357.
4. Private information.
5. Wheeler-Bennett, George VI, pp. 312–13.
6. Alan Don, Diary 10/12/36 (Lambeth Palace Library).
7. Ziegler, Edward VIII, p. 382.
8. Wheeler-Bennett, George VI, p. 380.

5. THE KING AT WAR

1. Rhodes-James, George VI, p. 170.
2. Ibid., p, 189.
3. Counting One's Blessings, p. 290.
4. Wheeler-Bennett, George VI, p. 446.
5. Rhodes-James, George VI, p. 195.
6. Ibid., p. 447.
7. Betty Spencer Shew, Queen Elizabeth The Queen Mother (London: Hodder & Stoughton, 1955), p. 76.
8. Rhodes-James, George VI, p. 548.
9. Ziegler, Mountbatten, p. 125.
10. Wheeler-Bennett, George VI, p. 520.
11. John G. Winant, A Letter from Grosvenor Square (London: Hodder & Stoughton, 1947), p. 19.
12. Winston Churchill, The Second World War, vol. 4 (London: Cassell, 1951), pp. 657–9.
13. Wheeler-Bennett, George VI, pp. 601–5.
14. R. J. Minney, Private Papers of Hore-Belisha (London: Collins, 1960), pp. 237–8.
15. Ziegler, Edward VIII, p. 412.
16. Ibid., p. 427.

6. THE FINAL YEARS

1. Ziegler, *Edward VIII*, p. 427.
2. *Counting One's Blessings*, p. 385.
3. Martin Gilbert, *Winston S. Churchill*, vol. 8 (London: Heinemann, 1988), p. 115.
4. Rhodes-James, *George VI*, p. 302.
5. Wheeler-Bennett, *George VI*, p. 662.
6. *Counting One's Blessings*, p. 470.
7. Ashley Jackson, *The British Empire and the Second World War* (London: A&C Black, 2006), p. 26.
8. Rhodes-James, *George VI*, p. 313.
9. Wheeler-Bennett, *George VI*, p. 320.
10. Philip Ziegler, *Crown and People* (London: 1978), p. 90.

Further Reading

The official life of King George VI, that by Sir John Wheeler-Bennett (London: Macmillan, 1958) is courteous, scholarly, perhaps a shade too deferential. Sarah Bradford's *George VI* (London: Weidenfeld & Nicolson, 1989) is the most substantial of the other biographies; it is exceptionally well written and entertaining. Robert Rhodes-James's *A Spirit Undaunted: The Political Role of George VI* (London: Little Brown, 1998), as the title suggests, concentrates on the official life. It is thoughtful and intelligent. Among other biographies are those by Denis Judd (London: Michael Joseph, 1982) and Patrick Howarth (London: Hutchinson, 1987).

Queen Elizabeth has been almost as well served. The excellent, if enormously long, official biography by William Shawcross (London: Macmillan, 2009) is complemented by Elizabeth Longford's *The Queen Mother* (London: Weidenfeld & Nicolson, 1981) and Hugo Vickers' informative *Elizabeth, the Queen Mother* (London: Random House, 2006). William Shawcross is also responsible for *Counting One's Blessings: The Selected Letters of Queen Elizabeth the Queen Mother* (London: Macmillan, 2012).

George VI's life is inevitably interwoven with the life of his elder brother, who reigned briefly as King Edward VIII and lingered on as Duke of Windsor till 1972. Frances Donaldson's *Edward VIII* (London: Weidenfeld & Nicolson, 1989) and Philip Ziegler's official biography (London: Collins, 1990) are probably the most consequential of the many books available. What promises to be a valuable book on the four royal princes, by Deborah Cadbury, will be published in 2015 under the title *Princes at War*.

The serious historical study of the modern British monarchy, going beyond the conventional reign-by-reign biographical treatment, and addressing broader themes and questions, is a relatively recent scholarly development. For two initial forays, see David Cannadine (who, in fact, is himself responsible for this paragraph), 'The Context, Performance and Meaning of Ritual: The British Monarchy and the "Invention of Tradition", c.1820–1977', in Eric Hobsbawm and Terence Ranger (eds), *The Invention of Tradition* (Cambridge: Cambridge University Press, 1983); and idem, 'The Last Hanoverian Sovereign? The Victorian Monarchy in Historical Perspective, 1688–1988', in A. L. Beier, D. Cannadine and J. M. Rosenheim (eds), *The First Modern Society: Essays in English History in Honour of Lawrence Stone* (Cambridge: Cambridge University Press, 1989). A perceptive study of the monarchy and national life in George V's day is Ross McKibbin, *Classes and Cultures: England 1918–1951* (Oxford: Oxford University Press, 1998), while Andrzej Olechnowicz (ed.), *The Monarchy and the British Nation, 1780 to the Present* (Cambridge: Cambridge University Press, 2007), is a fine recent collection of essays. For particular subjects, see Vernon Bogdanor, *The Monarchy and the Constitution* (Oxford: Clarendon Press, 1995); Philip Hall, *Royal Fortune: Tax, Money and the Monarchy* (London: Bloomsbury, 1992); Frank Prochaska, *Royal Bounty: The Making of a Welfare Monarchy* (New Haven, CT: Yale University Press, 1995); and James Loughlin, *The British Monarchy and Ireland, 1800 to the Present* (Cambridge: Cambridge University Press, 2007).

Picture Credits

1. Prince Albert in a sailor suit
2. The official engagement photograph of the Duke of York and Lady Elizabeth Bowes-Lyon
3. The Prince of Wales and the Duke of York out with the Belvoir Hunt
4. At Wimbledon, 1923, partnered by Louis Greig
5. At Glamis, 1927
6. The Duke and Duchess of York at Sandwich with Princess Elizabeth and Princess Margaret Rose, 1932
7. With General Eisenhower in North Africa, June 1943
8. In Malta, June 1943
9. With President Roosevelt, Washington, 1939
10. With Winston Churchill, 8 May 1945
11. One of the last photographs of the king, late November 1951

(All illustrations come from the Royal Collection Trust and are reproduced by gracious permission of Her Majesty the Queen)

Index